DEDICATION

Dedicated to my pastor, mentor, and friend,
Dr. Jim Diehl.

He taught me how to "see"
with eyes of faith.

SUCH GREAT FAITH

YOU CAN HAVE FAITH
THAT MOVES MOUNTAINS

DANNY GODDARD

dustjacket

◆dustjacket

w w w . d u s t j a c k e t . c o m

TABLE *of* CONTENTS

ACKNOWLEDGEMENTS

*I thank my God
every time I remember you.*
(Philippians 1:3, NIV)

St. Paul was extremely grateful for his friends in the church at Philippi. They were there for him in a time of great need. His epistle to the Philippians is nothing more than a four-chapter thank you note. As I have written this book on faith, I feel somewhat like the apostle, for I, too, am extremely thankful for many people who have helped me along the journey.

First of all, I must thank my wife, Sandie, and my son and daughter-in-law, Tommy and Micha. They have always been my biggest boosters and continue to encourage me to write. Most of our family vacations turn into writing sessions for me but they don't seem to mind (much). I appreciate Sandie proofing my manuscript and suggesting some changes and making corrections.

I also must thank Dr. Jim Diehl, General Superintendent Emeritus in the Church of the Nazarene. He came into my life as my pastor just after my Dad had died and Pastor Diehl became my mentor. Dr. Diehl did more than teach me how to make a hospital call, write a sermon outline, and give an altar call—he taught me how to be a person of faith. He taught me how to develop the eyes of a preacher and to see spiritual lessons in all that surrounds me.

Throughout life we have many acquaintances and a few good friends. General Superintendent, Dr. David Graves, has been a great friend. He and I began pastoring together about the same time on the North Carolina District under the tremendous leadership of Dr. Bill Sullivan, and we have since served together in the area of Sunday School ministries. I am honored that Dr. Graves has written the foreword for this book.

My sincere appreciation goes to my congregation, that of First Church of the Nazarene in New Castle, Indiana. It has been the privilege of Sandie and me to pastor this church for the past six years, and I feel that those good people believe in me.

Finally, I thank God Who has not only given me great experiences of faith but has also displayed His hand in my life so that others may see. Again and again He has proven to me that He is bigger than what's the matter! To God be the glory for such great faith that not only can be mine but can also be yours.

Danny Goddard
New Castle, IN

FOREWORD

The words "faith" and "believe" appear almost five hundred times in the New Testament, suggesting that these qualities have a significant role in living the Christian life. Even before the story of Abraham, God's Word plainly tells us that "without faith it is impossible to please God, for whoever would approach him must believe that he exists and that he rewards those who seek him" (Hebrews 11:6, NRSV).

With a biblical and pastoral approach, my friend, Danny Goddard, writes about this critical subject in his new book, *Such Great Faith*. As a pastor for more than three decades, Goddard has regularly faced issues of faith within his congregations. The book is filled with personal vignettes that illustrate the eternal truth that faith is not optional but mandatory for every child of the King. Stories from Goddard's life and ministry journey—even spiritual lessons from his golden retriever, Dolly—bring humor and light to his writing.

Goddard has learned the adventurous life of faith while trusting God for the impossible, and he challenges us to:

Crawl out on a limb of faith, out on to the tiny branches. Take a risk. Believe Him for a miracle. Put all your trust in the only One Who can catch you, should you fall. Dream some big dreams. Allow God to be God. Become a successful Christian as well as a faithful one. Believe in your heart of hearts that He really is bigger than what's the matter. Put all of this together and you have Such Great Faith.

Goddard's book will help your God become bigger and your faith to increase.

I pray that God will give you the desires of your heart with this endeavor, and that many believers will be encouraged and challenged to step by faith into all He has in store for them.

Blessings,
David W. Graves
General Superintendent, Church of the Nazarene

INTRODUCTION

WHATEVER HAPPENED TO FAITH?

And without faith
it is impossible to please God
(Hebrews 11:6, NIV)

I once preached a series of sermons that I called, *Whatever Happened To ...* Each message took my congregation back to yesteryear, back to the day when certain spiritual subjects were evidently more important than they are today. Topics included "Whatever Happened to the Blood?", "Whatever Happened to the Lord's Day?", "Whatever Happened to Growing in Grace?", "Whatever

Happened to a Crisis Experience?", "Whatever Happened to Praying Through?", and, oh yes, "Whatever Happened to Faith?"

Although a third generation Nazarene and raised in the faith, I was away from church and from God for four of my teenage years. On Sunday night, November 5, 1972 at the age of nineteen, much to the delight of my family, the prodigal finally returned, experiencing a new birth, and beginning a journey with Jesus, an expedition that definitely included something called *"faith."*

During my growing up years, I had sung all the hymns, heard all the sermons, and learned all the ecclesiastical lingo. I knew what it was to *"surrender one's all to Jesus."* I understood the intentions of those who told seekers at an altar of prayer to *"let go and let God."* I didn't have to think twice about what it meant to *"pray through."* Yet I was at a place in my newfound Christian life to where I needed no more clichés or church jargon, I just needed Jesus. I was so hungry for something or Someone Who was really real, something or Someone Who could reach me where I was, something or Someone Who would help me to stay straight in a crooked world. In short, I wanted to see answers to prayer, I longed to experience miracles in my life, and I needed so desperately to sense the Presence of the Lord, as did the priests when they could not enter the temple because of the overwhelming glory of God! (2 Chronicles 7:2) What I needed was faith, not just a half-hearted belief in God, but a sincere, genuine assurance to believe that He actually can and will do what the Scriptures say He can and will do. For the first time in my life I wanted and needed to truly depend upon God.

As you will read in this book's first chapter, I was called to preach in a wrestling ring, though I didn't recognize it as such at the time. I walked away from a somewhat promising career as a pro wrestling referee to attend college six years after high school. Though I felt I was definitely Spirit-led, everywhere I turned the word *"impossible"* flashed in neon across my world. Ann Kiemel's book, *I Love the Word Impossible,* helped me tremendously, no, it inspired and motivated me to really get out on a limb and trust God with all that was within me.

Almost four decades have passed and I am still trying my best to defeat doubt and exercise great faith. It concerned me a few years ago, however, when I heard of a young pastor-friend who was offered three churches at once by a district superintendent and asked, "Which do you think would be the best fit for you?" For me, that would just be confusing. I guess I'm still romantic enough to believe there is only one specific place that God has for me at a particular time. I have a hard time believing that God's Will for a minister is his or her choice of door number one, door number two, or door number three.

It also bothers me to hear that some of today's pastors send out resumes to superintendents by the boatloads, as if applying for a job. I realize this is a different day and church leaders and boards have to work with resumes. I certainly have no problem sending one when requested, but I've never just sent out my resume when the going got tough. My thought has always been that God knows where I am, and He knows my situation. Instead of sending out pleas, I'm more inclined to send up prayers! I'll readily admit that there have been times in my ministry when I wondered if God had forgotten me, yet I always truly felt that if He wanted to move me, He would make it happen—and He always has.

Never will I forget that Thursday in November when Sandie and I arrived in the midwest to begin our second pastorate. We had driven our car and a twenty-foot yellow rental truck for four days from North Carolina to Nebraska to pastor a church we had accepted over the phone, sight unseen. A small district in the early eighties, the Nebraska District had no funds to bring a prospective pastor in for an interview so all we had to rely upon was the Lord Himself. We were on our faces before God for several days until we received certain direction regarding His will.

In his book, *Fresh Faith,* Jim Cymbala writes:

> *In today's church, we have a serious shortage of faith in a living, speaking God. Pastors and laity alike do not seem to believe that God really leads and directs. Research by George Gallup shows that fewer than 10 percent of church-going Christians make important life decisions based on God's Word and seeking His Will! In other words, more than 90 percent decide on the basis of their own intelligence, peer opinion, whim, or fancy. They marry people and move to new cities without so much as a ten-minute prayer. Yet every Sunday they sit in a church pew singing songs like 'Where He leads me, I will follow.'[1]*

Having sat on the board that credentials ministers, my fear is that young pastors are entering the ministry not really having experienced a personal encounter with faith, much less a genuine Call of God. It concerns me that some laypeople are living out their Christian lives without any knowledge of what it means to get out on a skinny limb of trust. It worries me to wonder if men and women of God still exercise a faith that moves mountains. I believe Jim Cymbala is dead on when he says that faith is something the devil wants to steal away from us all.[2] Allow that to happen, and we can never ever please our Creator. (Hebrews 11:6)

I have always looked at Hebrews chapter 11 as "God's Hall of Fame," but perhaps a better description would be "God's Hall of Faith." The men and women whose names are listed in that roster are those who exercised tremendous faith in a God Who is bigger. Abel, Enoch, Noah. They knew what it meant to trust God when they were backed against the wall. Abraham, Isaac, Jacob. They understood that the power of Almighty God was all they had going for them. Joseph, Moses, Rahab. They left everything behind, some of them having no idea where they were headed. Each one is introduced with phrases like *"by faith"* or *"through faith."* Then in verse 32, other names are added to the list: Gideon, Barak, Samson, Jephthah, David, Samuel, and Danny. (The last one, my own addition)

Today I am so thankful that, as I have sought God over the decades, He has always responded with divine direction. It is my prayer that this book, filled with my own personal stories, might inspire and motivate a Christian somewhere to become completely dissatisfied until he or she has seen the glory of God. (Exodus 33:18) In my own personal journey I have truly learned that "I can do all things through Christ Jesus." (Philippians 4:13, NKJV)

In his book about our quest for holiness discipleship, Dr. Frank Moore wrote: "Expect to be amazed. There are many things in life I don't know or understand. But one thing I'm sure of: God will amaze you when you embark on a quest of discovery with Him."[3] I say, let's embark!

Danny Goddard
New Castle, Indiana

CHAPTER ONE

CALLED to PREACH in a WRESTLING RING

You will hear a voice behind you saying,
"This is the way. Follow it"
(Isaiah 30:21, GW)

I was about six years old when my Dad started taking me to the professional wrestling matches at the Atlanta City Auditorium. What began as an occasional event soon became a weekly activity on Friday nights. While my schoolmates could name ballplayers and quote batting averages and touchdowns scored, I could tell you the names of pro wrestlers, their hometowns, and their finishing holds. I knew that Joe Scarpa was from Mobile, Alabama and used the abdominal stretch; Tarzan Tyler hailed from Seattle, Washington and used the backbreaker; and the Mysterious

Masked Medics, dressed in medicinal-white masks, boots, and tights, came from parts unknown and used whatever they could to distract the referee and win the bout.

One particular week, in order to accommodate a huge crowd, the Atlanta matches were moved to the old Ponce de Leon Ballpark, home of the Atlanta Crackers. During intermission, I left my seat in the bleachers to run down to the locker room area in hopes of getting a glimpse of the famous Argentina Rocca, who was in town for the main event. Instead, the door suddenly flew open and out came Rocca's opponent for the evening, the hated and arrogant Sputnik Monroe! One of the most detested "bad guys" in the business, Monroe had been packing out arenas all over the South. Fans spent their hard-earned money in hopes of seeing him take a beating. I froze as he strutted past me on his way to the ring, glancing down at me with a snarl on his face. Never will I forget how that villain of the ring frightened me that night, but neither would I have ever thought that forty-some years later I would board a jet in Oklahoma City, fly to Louisiana, and preach his funeral.

It all started with a "change of heart." Monroe turned from a *"heel"* or *"bad guy,"* to a *"baby face"* or *"good guy,"* becoming much loved and approachable by the fans. I was about twelve years old when I introduced myself to him and shortly became president of the Sputnik Monroe Fan Club. Not long thereafter, Monroe moved to Florida to do the *"bad guy"* thing all over again. Back in the cable-less sixties, pro wrestlers could perform their *"angles"* yet again in various states, unknown to the fans outside the TV viewing area. Sputnik and I kept in touch through the mail and a year or so later, my Dad took me to Florida for a visit. On a couple of afternoons, while my Dad visited his parents who lived in a nearby town, I crawled into a gray station wagon with some of the most hated wrestlers in Florida: Sputnik and Rocket Monroe, their manager, Gentleman Saul Weingeroff, and Wild Bill Dromo. We drove from Tampa to Eau Gallie and back for the matches one night and then to Jacksonville and back the next.

Forever etched in my memory is how we hurriedly left the Jacksonville Coliseum with squalling tires as heated wrestling fans hurled Coke bottles toward our car! It was that night during a pit stop that Rocket Monroe asked me to hold something for them and he laid two heavy gold World Tag Team Championship belts in my lap! In the wee hours of the morning, I snoozed under those trophies all the way back to Tampa—quite an exciting experience for a thirteen-year old boy.

Throughout my teen years, I continued going to the wrestling cards in Atlanta, riding the city bus whenever my Dad was unable to get off work. When I began to drive at age sixteen, I took up photography as a hobby, shooting pictures of the matches with a Minolta 35mm camera. Within a few years, I advanced to a Yashica twin lens reflex with a strobe and battery pack to freeze the action, eventually landing the job of photographer for Georgia Championship Wrestling. Travelling the state of Georgia, I shot action pictures for the official program, *The Ringsider*. Occasionally, I would travel to St. Louis, Detroit, or Miami on planes with Rip Hawk or Dick the Bruiser to shoot pictures for wrestling magazines out of New York. Wrestlers such as Les Thatcher, Jerry Lawler,

Rocky Johnson, Abdullah the Butcher, and others became my friends and I even started working out with a few at local gyms.

Having grown up around pro wrestling, my secret desire had always been to become a wrestler myself but there was one huge deterrent: I was only a skinny 118 pounds! Taking me on as his personal project, wrestler Kevin Sullivan taught me holds, moves, and flips. He also tried to "fatten" me up with milkshakes, wheat germ, and banana splits, but nothing worked. After realizing I could never be a wrestler, it was suggested I become a referee. The ref is the one who carries the match and occasionally gets into the action himself, so I would be able to use some of the maneuvers I had learned. Unfortunately, there was no shortage of referees in the Georgia National Wrestling Association office and I was unknown elsewhere. Pro wrestling is one of those businesses where it matters greatly who you know.

One of the wrestlers for whom I had the greatest respect was my hooded friend, the masked Mr. Wrestling, Tim Woods. Knowing he had connections all over the country and that he could help me break into the business, I approached the masked grappler backstage one night at the City Auditorium and explained my plight. Tim's answer, however, angered me. He told me he could call the wrestling office in New Orleans or Charlotte or Mobile or a number of other places and get me started as a referee but that he would not do so because he felt I was *too nice a guy!* Looking back later, I realized Tim was trying to protect me and keep me out of a rough and crooked business, evidently seeing potential in me for something better.

Still determined to referee, I had another friend in the business, Jim Bell, who had made a deal to go wrestle in northeastern Ohio as the Masked Assassin. Aware of my dream, Jim also made arrangements to bring me along as a ref. Promised twice the money I had been making full time at Sears, I quit my job of six years and, listening to an 8-track tape of oldies music on a car stereo, I headed to Ohio with my hooded buddy to seek my fortune.

Working out of Youngstown, I reffed matches in Ohio for two weeks. A pro wrestling official isn't there to gain popularity, and I really got the heat stirred up with the fans because I didn't always "see everything" that took place in the ring. To my enjoyment, one wrestling fan called me a *"jive turkey referee!"* I was loving every minute! My career of glamour was short-lived, however, after two weeks of doing the work, yet neither one of us saw a dime of the promised pay. Though I was having the time of my life, we returned home where I was able to get my photography job back at the big arenas but also started refereeing at some spot shows in the smaller towns with an independent group of wrestlers.

Now all this time I was striving to live a Christian life. Still a fairly new convert, I was walking in all the light I had, and I was trying to be an influence on the guys in the dressing rooms. One Fall evening in 1975, I was reffing in a ballpark in LaGrange, Georgia and it was intermission before the main event. The promoter sent me to the dressing room of the *"good guy,"* Randy Rose (who later found fame as half of the tag team, "The Midnight Express") to tell him that he would win the Southern Heavyweight Championship that night.

He was to be pinned for a two-count, kick out, catch the champ off the ropes and roll him up into a *"small package"* for the pin and the win. Randy was elated!

As I headed to the locker room of the villains to clue-in Rose's opponent on the plan, I was stopped just outside the door by the promoter, the Masked Assassin. He told me to tell the champ, Bobby Best, that he would pin Rose, but instead of Randy kicking out after a two-count, I was to give him a fast count, give the win to Best, and we were to get out of there as fast as we could! This would be a terrible surprise for Rose but the boss, a wrestler himself, felt like Randy was taking on an attitude and we were going to *"teach him a lesson!"*

The match began and I had trouble concentrating. I felt like I was deceiving my friend, Randy Alls (real name), but then it dawned on me that I had been deceiving the fans all along. As if for the first time, I *"heard"* the curse words that were screamed at me by the crowd. Then I heard a Voice somewhere inside my head that seemed to whisper, "I've got something better for you than this!"

Rose and Best continued to wrestle while I grappled with staying focused. The timekeeper periodically inform-ed me as to how much time had lapsed and it was soon time to go into the finish. I whispered to the wrestlers, "Let's take it home," the signal to begin their finishing moves. At that point I again heard that Voice, "I've got something better for you than this!" Amid the boos of the crowd, the hated bad guy pinned Randy, who understood he was going to kick-out after a two-count. But to Randy's surprise, I counted one, then a quick two and three together! We all jumped to our feet. I motioned to the timekeeper to ring the bell. He tossed the championship belt through the ropes to me, and I slapped it against Best as I quickly raised his arm in victory. Emotions exploded! Irate fans stormed the ring! Randy Rose was furious! The bleached blonde Bobby Best and I hurriedly slid under the bottom rope, and we were immediately surrounded by several Georgia State Patrolmen, who safely escorted us through the angry mob and back to the dress-ing room.

We were locked in the locker room that night until the ballpark had cleared. Arrests had been made of drunken fans armed with knives. I didn't go to the shower that evening. Instead, I sat in a corner, still in my striped shirt and wrestling shoes. I listened as the wrestlers told their usual off-color jokes and used language that should be offensive to any Christian. Then I heard it a third time, that inner Voice that seemed to keep echoing in my mind: "I've got something better for you than this!"

A state patrolman knocked on the door and gave us the "all clear." I left the building that night, got into my still fairly new 1974 Pontiac Fire Bird, and headed for Atlanta. Looking up at a beautiful star-speckled Georgia sky, I prayed, assuring God that I truly wanted His will for my life instead of my own. I told Him that if He did have something better for me, then that's exactly what I needed and that's what I wanted. On that October Thursday evening on a lonely Georgia interstate somewhere between LaGrange and Atlanta, I surrendered pro wrestling to Jesus. The following Sunday night after church, I got into a car with my pastor, Dr. Bennett Dudney, and we made the 250-mile trip to Nashville. The next day I toured the campus of Trevecca Nazarene College, the school my pastor had been encouraging me to attend.

It didn't take long for me to fall in love with Trevecca. By January, six long years after high school, I was a full-time college student, something to which I had never aspired. That Voice continued to ring in my brain, but I wasn't sure if God was speaking or if I was just on a spiritual high. Finally, six months after God had spoken to me in a Georgia wrestling ring, I went to an altar at an Atlanta revival meeting as a college student and accepted God's call to preach.

Being extremely shy, this, for me, was truly an act of faith. Back in high school, I would gladly accept an undesirable grade, rather than give a book report before my peers. Struggling with this new call on my life, I found assurance in the Scriptures and read in my Bible about Moses. He didn't hear a call of God in a wrestling ring, but He heard it from a burning bush. God wanted Moses to be His mouthpiece to Pharaoh in order to free the Israelites from Egyptian bondage. The passage really got my attention when Moses was explaining to God that he was not a good speaker, to which the Lord replied, "Who hath made man's mouth? or who maketh the dumb, or deaf, or the seeing, or the blind? have not I the Lord? Now therefore go, and I will be with thy mouth, and teach thee what thou shalt say." (Exodus 4:11-12, KJV) Eight years later, I would open my Bible to this very passage and place my hands upon it, as Dr. Eugene Stowe, General Superintendent, ordained me an elder in the Church of the Nazarene.

I promised the Lord that I would preach anywhere, and it wasn't long before I received my first invitation. Having been given my name for pulpit supply, the Nazarene pastor at Covington, Georgia called and invited me to come. Remembering my promise to God, I accepted the challenge. Now to this point, I had not attended any classes on homiletics or hermeneutics or anything to do with preaching. I had been working on church history, speech, Greek, and racquetball. My pastor, Rev. Jim Diehl, taught me how to write a sermon outline, and I depended upon the Holy Spirit to help me prepare a message. That Sunday morning in Covington, I stood before that congregation with fear and trembling and preached my very first sermon. I was so glad the pulpit was there, for it not only gave me something on which to hold, but it also hid my right leg that began to shake uncontrollably, as if it had a mind of its own! Now I look back on that first sermon outline and realize how theologically incorrect it was, but the Holy Spirit used it anyway and people seemed to get spiritual help at the altar.

For a young ministerial student, this was only the beginning of a life of total dependence upon God. It wasn't easy for me to just hop on to the faith wagon. I was hit with doubt just like everyone else. Dr. Tony Evans says, "Sometimes faith and doubt get mixed together in our minds."[1] I began to read everything I could get my hands on that might bring encouragement. Almost immediately, I became aware that some pastors were discouraged and had taken on an "I-don't-care" attitude. I've since read that "Apathy is often a symptom of anemic faith," therefore, I have to be always about protecting my faith.[2]

Four pastorates into my ministerial career, I noticed that the Muncie, Indiana newspaper was advertising a pro wrestling card at Monroe Central High School. The main event featured my old friend and wrestling trainer, Kevin Sullivan. It had been almost twenty years since we had talked. With Kevin being that close, I decided to drive over to Parker City that afternoon and wait in the parking lot just to see him. Arriving early, I watched as various wrestlers drove up and made their way into the high school building. Finally, a carpool of *"bad guys"* arrived and, among them, I recognized my old pal. Over the years, I had seen on TV that Kevin had become one of the *"heels"* and had done a good job of being bad, making the fans all over the country detest him.

Kevin and the masked *"One Man Gang"* were getting their gear out of the trunk of the car when I approached and politely addressed my friend, "Kevin?" Without looking my way, Sullivan, in his villainous character, growled in his gruff wrestler's voice, "Yeah?" I decided I wasn't going to be treated like a *"mark,"* or mere wrestling fan, so I waited in silence. When I didn't respond, he looked up and I put out my hand, reminding him, "Danny Goddard." The facial expression of the policeman standing by showed surprise when, not only did Kevin Sullivan's countenance change, but so did his voice to a friendlier tone! "Danny! What are you doing here?" I told him I was now a pastor and lived nearby. He said he had heard that in a dressing room in some arena one night and that he was so happy for me. He asked if I was coming inside but I told him I didn't have a ticket and hadn't been to a wrestling match in a long, long time. Refusing to take no for an answer, he insisted I come in with him through the back door, and so we followed the police officer inside.

Kevin had to get his instructions for the evening and told me he would be out later and we could talk, so I went to the foyer and peeked into the gym. The bleachers were full of people and many were sitting in folding chairs on the floor at ringside. The bell rang to signal the *"curtain raiser,"* or opening match. The wrestlers and referee climbed into the ring, and I heard the boos and jeers and even the curse words hurled toward the referee. Suddenly, it all came back on me, and then I *"heard"* it—that Voice within whispered the words I had not heard in many years: "I've got something better for you than this!"

Asking God for forgiveness, I hurried out the nearest exit door, scribbled a note on the back of my business card, and left it on my friend's car. Pro wrestling may not be a sin for anyone else but it is for me because that's from whence I was delivered. I left that high school that evening feeling good that I had seen my friend again; I drove into Muncie and got the biggest pizza I could find! I thank God for bringing me from where I once was, and I thank Him for faith to believe He indeed had *"something better."* Might He have something better for you? If so, it will take great faith to go from where you are to where God wants you to be.

CHAPTER TWO

The GET-OUT-ON-A-LIMB KIND of FAITH

Trust in the Lord with all your heart, and
lean not on your own understanding.
In all your ways acknowledge Him,
and He shall direct your paths.
(Proverbs 3:5-6, NKJV)

As I had mentioned in the previous chapter, Pastor Bennett Dudney did his best to persuade me to enroll at Trevecca Nazarene College, now University, in Nashville, Tennessee. Without applying a lot of pressure, he would occasionally ask me to pray about it. In my thinking, college was completely out of the question. First of all, I had never planned on a college career and it had been almost six years since I had graduated from high school. An institution of higher learning probably wouldn't even have me! Secondly, even if I was somehow accepted, I couldn't afford the tuition. My Dad was paying the bills for my younger sister, already a freshman at TNC, and I knew there were no funds left for me. The final reason that kept me out of school was that I had some mounting credit card debt and a brand new car with payments 'til Jesus comes. Why would I even attempt to pray about such? For me, college was for sure, an impossibility.

At the same time, I had come to a place in my life where I was tired of floundering. I had flipped hamburgers, pumped gas, worked in a grocery store meat department, photographed weddings, and I was presently working at the old Sears catalog distribution center near downtown Atlanta. I had been there for six years and I hated my job. It was the same old thing, working in the packing aisle, day in and day out. On the side, I was shooting pro wrestling pictures and had just started refereeing in small towns in the evenings. Someone said you'll never make a change until you get *"sick and tired of being sick and tired!"* That's where I was back in 1975 at the age of twenty-two.

Following that God-experience in a Georgia wrestling ring that October Thursday evening (chapter 1), I really meant the prayer I prayed as I drove home. More than anything in the world, I wanted God's Will for my life and I truly had surrendered everything to Him on that unforgettable night. Only a three year old Christian, I suddenly found my spiritual life growing quite rapidly. Since leaving my wrestling career behind, I now had to decide where to go and what to do. I immediately phoned my pastor and explained my quandary. He again asked if I had prayed about TNC, and I hadn't, but now my full-time job was no longer an excuse. I had resigned at Sears some months before to go to Ohio to referee, a job that lasted all of two weeks. Now jobless and with a new car to support, I was forced to begin to seriously pray about Trevecca Nazarene College. In the meantime, Dr. Dudney made plans to personally drive me to Nashville the very next Sunday evening after church.

We made the five-hour trip, arriving at a motel very late that night. The next morning after breakfast, we went straight to the President's office at TNC. Dr. Mark R. Moore was out of town, but Pastor Dudney introduced me to Dr. Harper Cole, second in command, then to Dr. Phil Storey, who was known on campus as "Pop" Storey, and also Dr. Bob Brower, another administrator. After touring the campus, I decided to linger most of the week to get a real "feel" for the school. My pastor returned home but I purchased a one-way return Greyhound bus ticket for four days later.

The more I prayed, the more I felt like Trevecca was the place God had in mind for me. My sister, Vickie, was already there as a freshman and so was Sandie Waldrep, my best friend from Atlanta, who eventually became my wife. Though I already had some investment there, I still needed clear direction from God. That's when I discovered Proverbs 3:5-6, "Trust in the Lord with all your heart, and lean not on your own understanding. In all your ways acknowledge Him, and He shall direct your paths." (NKJV)

Only twenty-two, I was tired. I was tired of hopping from job to job. I was tired of professing to know God without really *"experiencing"* God. I was tired of having no meaning, no purpose, nothing to which I could look forward. I was tired of acknowledging a personal relationship with God but not allowing Him to actually move in my life. Oswald Chambers wrote, "If a person is ever going to do anything worthwhile, there will be times when he must risk everything by his leap in the dark."[1] With that concept in mind, I returned to Atlanta and finally prayed through. It was October when I made the decision to enroll at TNC, sending in all the paperwork to begin school in January. Within a month, I received a letter of acceptance and suddenly realized, I was headed for Music City! As I continued to seek God, I also began to study that verse I had found in Proverbs. It calls for three things on the part of any believer …

WE ARE TO TRUST HIM

The Scripture says we are to trust God with all of our hearts. Part of our heart won't do, nor will most of it. We are to trust Him explicitly, with all that is within us. The Message translates, "from the bottom of your heart." Even the Psalmist said, "It is better to put trust in the Lord than to put confidence in man." (Psalm 118:9, NKJV) With my application to college, combined with a later letter of acceptance, I had crawled out on a limb!

Profit sharing received from my six-year stint at Sears quickly paid off my credit card balance. School, however, was still a financial impossibility, since I had absolutely no funds for tuition and I still had thirty-six sizeable monthly car payments left. But again, I had come to a place in my journey where I was so weary of a shallow commitment to Christ. Therefore, I decided to really trust Him for the first time in my life. I started to pray about how I would make those car notes while studying full time, but the answer that seemed to flash across my mind was one I had not consider-ed, nor wanted to hear: *"Sell the car!"*

Now this was one to ponder for awhile. This wasn't just any car. We're talking about a brand new 1974 Pontiac Firebird, the one I had purchased off the showroom floor. It was a beautiful silver with shiny black interior. I used to keep the seats waxed down and the car *"all gussied-up,"* as my daughter-in-law, Micha, would say. I even went by the handle, *"Silver Bird,"* on the CB radio and I would play a Mark Lindsey tape singing *"Silver Bird, fly my baby away"* as I would cruise through Shoney's late at night. *"Anything, Lord, except getting rid of my car!"*

But the more I sought God's guidance, the more the Lord seemed to remind me of my late-night promise made from a Georgia interstate, and so I put a "For Sale" sign in the window—only one sign—a small one—a really small one—in a back passenger window. Realizing I wasn't doing my best to sell that car, I drove out to Plaza Pontiac, the place of its purchase. Still very much a kid in those days, I had wanted to do my own thing without help from my Dad or anyone else and now, eighteen months later, they were telling me that I owed too much to get out of it. They were unable to give me what I needed in order to pay off the loan. I was *"upside down"* in my vehicle, but for the first time in my life I was also *"out on a limb"* of faith, trusting a God Who is bigger than what's the matter! I was not going to give up.

Reading our denominational magazine one day, the *Herald of Holiness,* I came across a great quote that I still remember to this present hour (though I don't recall which issue): "Often when God is going to do a wonderful thing, He begins with a difficulty. When He is going to do a very wonderful thing, He begins with an impossibility." I thought, *"That's exactly what I have—an impossibility!"* I was now more determined than ever to get rid of that Firebird and get on with college life.

Unfortunately, I didn't get much help at home. My Dad's health had forced him into early retirement and he was pretty much homebound, suffering from diabetes and kidney disease. Almost apologetically, he tried to explain that he didn't see how he could pay for my college since my younger sister, Vickie, was already there. Interrupting, I assured him it was alright because God was going to provide the means. As if the lack of money was not enough, more obstacles quickly presented themselves. I had friends, even a few family members, who said it was not a good idea for me to go to Nashville. Some said there was no way financially I would be able to stay and that I would be back soon with a huge bill. One close relative said that I had never finished anything before and he wondered how long I would stick with this new endeavor. All of these comments were very hurtful, but I was not going to be deterred.

Thankfully, I did have a few supporters. I had support from Gideon. I read how God had called him to defeat the marauding Midianites as one man. (Judges 6:15-16) I received encouragement from teenaged Mary, realizing that, with no help from a man, she was chosen from all the ladies in the land to be the mother of the Christ Child, an event that was to be a virgin birth! (Luke 1:34-37) I was pumped from Paul, the God-filled apostle who wrote to the Philippian Church: "I can do all things through Christ who strengthens me." (Philippians 4:13, NKJV) The more biblical stories I read, the better I became at trusting God. I was trusting God.

WE ARE TO ACKNOWLEDGE HIM

The verse in Proverbs not only says we are to trust God, but it also says that we are to acknowledge Him in all our ways, that is, give Him glory for everything (Proverbs 3:6). Jim Newheiser explains: "We are not merely to acknowledge God's lordship over our religious life; we are to bring God's truth to bear on every aspect of life. We trust him in how we run our families, our education, our careers, our finances, and our friendships. He is Lord of all!"[2]

That's what young David did as he went out to slay a giant: "... the Lord who delivered me from the paw of the lion, and from the paw of the bear, he will deliver me from the hand of this Philistine." (1 Samuel 17:37, NKJV) Just before his victory on Mount Carmel, the prophet Elijah prayed that all the people would know Who was God indeed. (1 Kings 18:38) Even as Jesus was about to raise Lazarus from the dead, He paused to publicly pray, "Father, thank you for hearing me. You always hear me, but I said it out loud for the sake of all these people standing here, so that they will believe you sent me." (John 11:41-42, NLT) Each of these individuals acknowledged that God was behind miraculous feats. It seemed that everywhere I turned, the barriers were up: "You can't afford to go to TNC! You have no money! How are you going to pay?" But my response was always the same:

God had called me to go and He would pay the way. Not only had I scooted out on a limb, but now I was swinging on the tiny branches!

One morning in early December, only three weeks away from my move to Nashville, I awoke with a start! Every attempt to sell my car had failed but on this particular morning I felt very strongly impressed to take my car back to Plaza Pontiac. I explained to the Lord (Who evidently had forgotten) that I had just done that a few weeks before. The impression was so strong, however, that I reluctantly agreed to do it again. I would come to understand that if God is in something, the idea or the desire to do a certain thing or to go in a specific direction will only grow stronger.

An hour later, I sat patiently across the desk from the car salesman who presented reason after reason as to why he was unable to offer me the amount of money I needed for my Firebird. He even allowed me to peek in his book that shows the top figures allowed for certain makes and models of cars. He shared the same from another book. Taking notice that he appeared to be struggling, I just sat in my seat and quietly prayed. Finally, the salesman sat back in his chair, looked at me, and said with almost an attitude of defeat, "Son, I'm gonna give you the money, but I don't know why!" For a few seconds, I thought I heard a choir of angels right there in the dealership singing the "Hallelujah Chorus!"

The papers were signed, the deal was made, the keys were turned over, and I went to a phone and called my sister for a ride home. Until she arrived, I sat on the curb at an auto dealership in Tucker, Georgia, and I praised my Creator—out loud! It was much like the shepherds after they had visited the Baby Jesus. Eugene Peterson says, "The sheepherders returned and let loose, glorifying and praising God." (Luke 2:20, MSG) I was definitely *"letting loose"* right there on a curb stone on the outskirts of Atlanta! Please understand, I was not happy about losing my car but I was immensely elated that God had actually proven Himself to me for the first time! No doubt about it, He had answered prayer.

Christmas 1975 came and went, rushing me to only a week before heading to Trevecca. My Dad was not feeling well enough to go to church that particular Sunday. Upon my return home from the evening service, I was met by my Grandmother at the front door, informing me that I needed to take my father to the hospital. I immediately went to him and asked if he wanted to go to the emergency room but he said no—that he wasn't going to make it through the night. It had only been two years since I had lost my Mom at the age of forty-nine. I certainly wasn't ready to lose my Dad, as well. He quickly changed the subject to church. "What did the pastor preach on tonight? Was anyone at the altar? Did anyone get saved?" I answered his questions and a few minutes later, Daddy got up from his recliner, started down the hallway, and collapsed. At the young age of 54, my Dad, the most faithful Christian I knew, was gone.

We had his funeral on Wednesday. I packed on Thursday. On Friday, I buried my face in the passenger window of Vickie's car and silently wept as my sister drove us to Trevecca. Looking back, I can clearly see the Hand of God in all the events of the week. Had my Dad lived another day, the funeral would have caused me to miss my first day of college. It was as if God had allowed my Dad to be with me right up until the last possible moment.

Still having no money to attend TNC, I continued to acknowledge God. As part of the registration process, I sat in the office of the financial director who wanted to know how I would pay for school. I told him as kindly, but as honestly as I could, "I don't know. God is going to pay the bill." By the end of the first quarter, three days before my bill was due, I received an unexpected letter from an insurance office in Atlanta with an enclosed check for over $4,000! Without my knowledge, my Dad had listed me as a beneficiary on a life insurance policy! Dr. Neil B. Wiseman, one of the first professors in my college experience, wrote: "The record is amazing—what seemed impossible has been accomplished. Little has become much. Small has grown to big. Tough has become tender. Across two millennia, God's power working through human beings has transformed apparent impossibilities into glorious victories."[3]

WE ARE TO FOLLOW HIM

We are to trust God, acknowledge Him, and there's one last thing: We are to follow Him. That insurance check paid my tuition for quite a while, but only became the first in a series of miracles as I continued to trust and acknowledge my Creator. Since our house was left to the three Goddard siblings, I was unable to get much financial assistance because legally, I owned a home. I did, however, qualify for a loan. I also got a job as the school photographer which put $400 on my bill each and every quarter. And God provided the finances through various other ways as I continued on my quest of following my Savior.

The scripture says that as long as we trust Him and acknowledge Him, He will direct our paths. (Proverbs 3:5-6) The Message translates verse 6: "Listen for God's voice in everything you do, everywhere you go; he's the one who will keep you on track." If He is going to lead us, direct us, and keep us on the right path, then we are going to have to follow. That's exactly what I did.

I had followed the Lord to Trevecca because I had felt so very strongly led. Back in October I began to wonder if God was calling me to preach, something I had shared only with my pastor. That *"feeling,"* that *"call,"* continued to grow stronger until several weeks after beginning classes with an "undecided" major, at a revival altar under the preaching of Dr. Talmadge Johnson, I accepted God's call to preach and I followed His direction into full-time ministry. Each time I was asked to address this group or preach in that church, I followed His leadership and counted it an honor to speak for Jesus. I have tried for more than three decades of full-time pastoral ministry to follow Him, right up until now, as I pursue His strong impression to write this book.

Jesus said, in Luke 9:23, "If anyone desires to come after Me, let him deny himself, and take up his cross daily, and follow Me." (NKJV) That's precisely what I was trying to do. I was putting my own agenda aside and tagging along after Jesus. I discovered that when one does that, the anointing and blessing of Almighty God is a given. It's all part of our *"get-out-on-a-limb kind of faith."* I trust that, as you read this book, you're doing some limb-swinging of your own.

CHAPTER THREE

FAITH THAT TAKES a RISK

*By faith Abraham obeyed when he was called
to go out to a place that he was to receive
as an inheritance. And he went out,
not knowing where he was going.*
(Hebrews 11:8, ESV)

Willy T. Ribbs made history in 1991. He was the first black racecar driver to qualify for and compete in the Indy 500. Pastoring in Indiana at the time, I watched his proud father as he was interviewed on Indianapolis TV news. He told how Willy had decided at the young age of four that he would race. He mentioned the tricycle track that had been set up in the house and how his boy *"never did hit the TV"* when he came around the corner of the living room on two wheels! Racing at Indy had been Willy's dream and it finally became his dream-come-true. Willy profoundly said, "If you want to make it, you can."[1]

Nazarene theologian, Dr. W.T. Purkiser defined *"faith"* as "man's response to God's revelation."[2] As God makes Himself known to us, either by the Voice of His Spirit or by His written Word, we react with believing, so much that we actually do something—we *"act"* on our faith. James reminds us that faith without works is dead faith. (James 2:17)

The words *"faith"* and *"believe"* appear almost five hundred times in the New Testament, suggesting that they evidently have a significant role in living the Christian life. One place where the word *"faith"* is vitally important is in the book of Hebrews, chapter 11, that great passage that displays God's "Hall of Faith." As I mentioned in the Introduction, the passage speaks of Noah, Moses, Abel, and others who not only believed *in* God but actually believed God to the point of obedience. As we scan through the roster of role models, I especially like the information given to us on Abraham. His story describes faith for us in more than one way ...

A FAITH THAT'S REQUIRED

God's Word plainly says even before we get to Abraham that "without faith it is impossible to please God, for whoever would approach him must believe that he exists and that he rewards those who seek him." (Hebrews 11:6, NRSV) This faith of believing something before it happens is not optional for the Christian, but is mandatory for every child of the King. As a matter of fact, I think the key word here is *"child."* It is extremely important that we develop and display a child-like faith. Children trust, they love, and they forgive. Toddlers may get into a knock-down, drag-out over a toy and then burst into tears of anger or at least, hurt feelings. Within minutes, however, they are back at play because they seem to have the ability to forgive and forget. Not only do they trust, but children also believe. Jesus told His disciples that the greatest person in His kingdom is a child: "unless you change and become like children, you will never enter the kingdom of heaven." (Matthew 18:3, NRSV)

A long time ago I drove my son to and from preschool in Farmland, Indiana, the beginning of "firsts" for Tommy. It was the first time he was away from Mom and Dad for hours at a time; the first time he attended school; the first time he was entrusted to teachers outside our church. I was always concerned that he might become anxious over whether or not I would be back to pick him up. As he would get out of the car in the morning, I would assure him (perhaps even "over" assure him) that I would be waiting in the car when preschool was over. Just before noon I would be back, early, parked in the line of cars driven by the other parents, and my eyes would scan the crowd of exiting children until they focused on my son. I noticed he always came out with a bounce in his step, a certain sign of confidence that his Mom or Dad would be there.

This is the kind of faith our Creator requires. As we go through life, we are bombarded by so many things. There will be storms and stains and sticky situations. There will be times of discouragement, disappointment, and despair.

We'll face setbacks, heartache, even the death of those we love. My favorite singing group of the '60s put it this way:

> Everyone's life is bittersweet, it's a door that opens wide; And no man can call himself complete til He sees it from both sides. This door swings both ways, it's marked "in" and "out." Some days you will want to cry and some days you will shout. This door swings both ways, it goes back and forth; In comes a southern breeze or a cold wind from the North.[3]

Life will come at us fast and hard, but through it all, we need not be afraid, for we know God has promised His presence. (Hebrews 13:5) Faith is required.

A FAITH THAT'S RIDICULED

"By faith Noah, when warned about things not yet seen, in holy fear built an ark to save his family." (Hebrews 11:7, NIV) Noah was another great godly man of faith. I believe he was severely ridiculed by his buddies for his ideas and actions. God told Noah to build this huge boat because, of all things, water was going to actually fall from the sky and flood the earth! Now we must understand, rain had never happened anywhere in the world. No one knew the difference between sprinkles and a downpour. The Scripture tells us that plants and vegetation were watered by a mist that sprayed from the ground. (Genesis 2:6) A suggestion of "rain" was a pretty far-fetched concept.

Dr. Albert Lown explains Noah's obedience in great detail:

> *The design was divinely given, but the task of construction was a human responsibility, staggering in its complexity and immensity. The gathering of materials and the building without normal dockyard facilities was a nightmare in itself. Add to this the new conception of waterproofing 'without within'; the number of decks and stalls needed; plus the air conditioning essential to prevent overpowering odours and disease—the 'upper window'—poetic, parable sentiment takes second place in the light of zoological hygiene and practical need.*
>
> *Noah had no answer to skeptics and critics concerning his strange craft, the site of building, the lengthening years of toil, and the seeming waste of man's energies and life. His was not to reason why, but to labour on in season and out of season. God had commissioned the formidable undertaking, and faith had embraced the project ...[4]*

It took one hundred and twenty years for Noah to complete his project, and God added seven days of mercy! Can you imagine the ribbing our boat-builder must have received during his enormous construction project? Have you ever thought of the comments and laughter that must have come from passersby in the neighborhood? A year passed then ten, then decades, a century! But nothing stopped Noah. A faithful servant, he was determined to please God. Noah just continued construction of his ship even though there was never a drop of rain. He kept at it, showing the "stuff" of which he was made.

Hebrews 11:8 says, "By faith Abraham obeyed when he was called to go out to the place which he would receive as an inheritance. And he went out, not knowing where he was going." I'm sure friends, even family, questioned his decision but it didn't hinder Abraham. He simply obeyed God.

You and I are no different than Abraham or Noah or any of the others listed in God's Hall of Faith. When we believe strongly that God has indeed spoken to us and has given us a task to perform, not everyone is going to understand, not even those to whom we are closest. They will snicker at us if we're saved, they'll criticize us if we tithe, and they'll call us "fanatics" if we pray for healing. We may be laughed at. We might even be pelted with hurtful words. Surely, we will be the point of discussion behind our backs. But that's alright because we do what we know we must. We're doing it for Jesus, One Who was incredibly misunderstood and ridiculed Himself.

Cruel Roman soldiers stripped Him of his garments and replaced them with a scarlet robe. They twisted a vine of thorns into a crown and cruelly forced it down upon His head, drawing blood. A reed was placed in His hand and He was sarcastically hailed as a king. (Matthew 27:27-31) Passersby blasphemed Him and even the religious leaders mocked Him from the foot of the cross. (Mark 15:29-32) If the Son of God received this kind of treatment in His own creation, why should we be treated differently? Why shouldn't our faith be tested? Our belief will definitely be ridiculed.

A FAITH THAT'S RISKY

When known as Abram, Abraham was God-called to leave his country, his kindred, and his father's house to go to a land that God would eventually "show" him. (Genesis 12:1) Never did the Lord mention distance, destination, or even direction. And so, at the age of seventy-five (Genesis 12:4), Abram gathered his personal belongings, his immediate family, a few friends and set out. The NIV says he went, "even though he did not know where he was going."

At times, when it might appear to others that I am lost while driving, I usually jokingly tell my passengers to start picking berries and making tourniquets. We'll surely need berries in order to survive and we'll need lots of tourniquets for snakebites. Hebrews 11:8 is a place in the Scriptures for Abraham to pick berries and make tourniquets! The Message translates: "When he left he had no idea where he was going." Any way you read it, it was a tremendous risk for our Jewish friend and his loved ones! God's ways don't always make sense!

I heard about a farmer who was sitting under a walnut tree. He looked at some nearby pumpkin vines and said to himself: "God is really foolish and inexperienced. He put big, heavy pumpkins on a frail vine and then He puts small walnuts on a tree with branches that can hold a man. Any man can do better than that!" Just then, a breeze dislodged a walnut which fell, hitting the knowledgeable farmer on the noggin! Rubbing his head, he thought: "It's a good thing there wasn't a pumpkin up there!" That little story amuses us but it drives home the truth. God knows exactly what He's doing!

When I felt definitely led of God to move five hours away from home to attend college six years after high school, what I exercised was risky faith. I had no money, no scholarships, no parents to pay my way. Logically, it made absolutely no sense. When Sandie and I signed the papers to purchase our first car, it was only because we had prayed half the night before. We were a bit anxious, for such a purchase was quite questionable. How would we make payments? When we left the sunny South for the winter wonderland of Nebraska to pastor a church, sight unseen, not even in a photograph, we wondered if we were doing the right thing. But God helped me make it through four years of college and He even provided a raise in pay that was exactly the amount of our monthly car note, and He gave us five years of meaningful ministry in the Midwest where we made friends for life. God always seems to honor faith that takes a risk.

As a kid, I loved the black and white TV shows (still do). I could watch *Leave It to Beaver*, *The Andy Griffith Show*, or *The Honeymooners* for hours at a time. One show I enjoyed was *Father Knows Best*. Whether it was little Kathy or teenaged Bud who was in trouble, they soon discovered that their Dad was constantly right. The same holds true for us and our Heavenly Father. Even when God's ways don't make sense, we always discover that He had a plan all along. We absolutely must learn this lesson of trust!

A FAITH THAT'S RUGGED

Even when we are truly trusting God and trying our best to stay on the straight and narrow, we are never promised smooth-sailing ahead. Abraham certainly had his share of troubles and even found himself interceding for Sodom and Gomorrah. At times David felt like the whole world was against him and everyone was saying that even God couldn't be of help! (Psalm 3:1-2) But then not everyone listed in God's Hall of Fame had *The Life of Riley* (another black and white TV show that I watched as a kid). Some were tortured, beaten, sawn in two, and killed by swords or stoning. The Bible says they were "destitute, persecuted, wandering in deserts and hiding in caves." (Hebrews 11:35-38) I think the message to us here is fairly clear: Our faith will definitely be opposed!

One of the churches we pastored was located directly across the street from Girard Park, a nice community ball field that included more than one baseball diamond. During the games in the summertime, beer was sold to the spectators in the bleachers. Since the city council had decided for whatever reason to address this at their next meeting, a city councilman called me on the phone and asked if our church had any kind of stand against alcohol consumption. He felt that, because of our location, our church should have a say in the matter, a gesture I did appreciate.

At his request (and that should be underscored), I wrote a letter to the council, quoting passages from our *Manual* that outlined our denominational stand against the use and abuse of alcohol. Well, the local newspaper got hold of that letter and the headline on the front page read, *"Nazarenes Against Beer in Girard Park!"* The article sounded like I had personally initiated a campaign in the city to ban booze at ballgames, when all I had done was respond to the politician's plea!

Though I had never mounted a soapbox at the ballpark and preached, I did stand behind our *Manual's* statements, for I am of the Nazarene faith, a faith that was personally challenged in our town over the next few weeks. For example, one day I opened my home mailbox at the end of our driveway to find, sitting among our bills, letters, and pizza coupons, a full uncovered cup of beer. I also opened the Saturday newspaper to discover that the entire column of the sports editor was about me, personally ripping me apart by name and telling me to go back to the South and leave them alone! I had suddenly become bad news in that town. As a matter of fact, when I finally I resigned a few years later to assume another church elsewhere, I left a campaign that I did start to rid the city of pornography. Later I heard that the very liberal ministerial alliance was glad to see me go!

Your faith will need to be rugged. This Christianity-thing is not for the faint-hearted, it's for the faith-hearted! Just take a look at David or Job or Gideon. Even Elijah was hiding under a broom tree, thinking he was the only person left in Israel who loved God. More than once God asked him, "What are you doing *here*, Elijah?" (1 Kings 19:9,13) I don't think He was necessarily meaning his location under a juniper tree. God was questioning the condition of his trust, his faith. What was he doing there, in that spiritual state of mind? Spiritually speaking, Elijah was definitely not where he was expected to be. You and I must have a faith that's rugged.

A FAITH THAT'S REWARDED

If it's going to be so rough, then why bother? Why not just give up, throw in the towel, just quit and go home? It's because Jesus is a Rewarder! Our faith never goes unnoticed, nor unrewarded. The Bible says, "Therefore, since we are surrounded by so great a cloud of witnesses, let us also lay aside every weight and the sin that clings so closely, and let us run with perseverance the race that is set before us, look-ing to Jesus the pioneer and perfecter of our faith ..." (Hebrews 12:1-2) He's the end, the Omega, the One Who makes our faith perfect. As the songwriter said, "It will be worth it all, when we see Jesus!"

St. Paul encourages us: "... being confident of this very thing, that He who has begun a good work in you will complete it until the day of Jesus Christ." (Philippians 1:6) One of my favorite passages is that of the apostle's words to the Christians at Corinth: "We are afflicted in every way, but not crushed; perplexed, but not driven to despair; persecuted, but not forsaken; struck down, but not destroyed." (2 Corinthians 4:7-9) We so often give up way too soon. We have to learn how to keep our eyes on the prize, or I should say, on the Prize-giver. Those who have gone before us have filled the unseen bleachers that surround us. They are cheering us on. They are telling us that we can make it. They are scream-ing that they did it and so can we. But the biggest Encourager, the greatest Supporter, the One Who really matters is cheering us on and that is the Lord Jesus Himself.

God doesn't save us, then pat us on the back and tell us to make it the best way we can! He directs us. He walks with us. He leads us. He helps us to make it all the way to the finish. That does not mean, however, that life will be easy. Christianity will cost us. We'll have to scoot out on some limbs, perhaps even some tiny branches, and really trust

God. My first district superintendent, Dr. Bill Sullivan once said, "You will probably not accomplish a great work for God until you move into the region of risk."[5] Dreaming about racing in the Indy 500 was a great risk for Willy T. Ribbs, but he eventually achieved his goal. Where are you on your journey with Jesus?

CHAPTER FOUR

A LITTLE TRAINING FROM a LITTLE TRAIN

> *The Lord, who saved me from the paw of the lion*
> *And from the paw of the bear, will save me from*
> *the hand of this Philistine."*
> (1 Samuel 17:37, NRSV)

Our church was facing a mighty mountain. It was our second pastorate, a church of about forty people. District Assembly was only a month away and our annual budgets had not been paid. I don't recall the amount owed, but it might as well have been a million dollars because we didn't have it! Our people had given and given and given until they were given out. We had just emerged from a three-and-half year lawsuit that was forcing us to pay a second time for our newly constructed building. (We had faithfully paid the contractor, who had failed to pay his sub-contractors. Then the contractor was diagnosed with a late stage of cancer and soon passed away. Prior to my arrival as pastor, our church leaders had not signed lien-waivers and, as allowed by state law, twelve sub-contractors sued us for $37,000. Half of them accepted a settlement we offered and the judge awarded in favor of three of the remaining six, one of them the largest lien, who threatened to *"turn that church into a dancehall!"*). There just was no money left and yet we still had district obligations at the close of the assembly year.

A very young pastor, I was feeling the weight of it all. I couldn't just forget it, wipe the slate clean, and start over with a new year of ministry. Oh, I know the "district police" were not going to come and beat our door down, demanding the money, but I also realized the district was counting on us to do our part. *"Budgets,"* or often referred to as *"Shares for Others,"* are a church's assigned assessment toward missions and other ministries outside our local church. It's the way the District Church of the Nazarene, comprised of many local congregations, functions. Somehow I had to lead our people in taking care of our remaining responsibility for others. We had to step up to the plate and be part of the team. We could not let our district church down. What were we going to do?

Praying in my study one Thursday morning over how we would meet the overwhelming need, I was struck with an idea. Assuming it was of the Lord, I left the church and drove a few blocks downtown to the public library. I hadn't really used a library since high school, and I was feeling somewhat lost. During college, I spent many hours in the library commentary or research sections but didn't need to find very many individual books. To locate a book back in my school days, we would search through the card catalog files using the ancient Dewey decimal system. Once we found the number assigned to the book, we could go to the exact section of the library and locate the publication on the shelf. Without a clue as to how to find a book in the eighties, I went to the librarian's desk and sought help. She needed the title of the work and the name of the author, and I happened to know both: *The Little Engine That Could,* written by Watty Piper and illustrated by Lois Lenski. It had been a childhood favorite.

Marion, the librarian (My name for my helper, borrowed from *The Music Man*), led me to a wall of publications in the children's section and ran her finger down the shelf until it stopped on Watty Piper's masterpiece. We were soon back at the main counter and checking the book out. Passing the time while waiting on her computer, she asked, "Is this book for your son or daughter?" I answered, "No ma'am. We don't have children." "Oh," she went on, "Is it for another child you know?" This time I answered, "No ma'am. It's for me." She looked at me with a puzzled appearance, but asked no further questions, and I offered no additional information. I kindly thanked her, took my book, and left.

I needed to find a place away from the telephone and other interruptions at the church. Since Sandie was at work and the parsonage was empty, I knew I could find peace and solitude at home, so that's where I headed. I poured a big glass of Georgia sweet iced tea, leaned back in my recliner, and, while my congregation thought I was barricaded in my study, carefully studying commentaries and word studies and doing the exegesis for powerful God-anointed messages for Sunday, I was actually at home reading Watty Piper's childhood classic, *The Little Engine That Could*. But who says I wasn't doing something spiritual?

Mister Piper tells the story of an engine that pulled railroad cars "filled full of good things for boys and girls."[1] The train was carrying colorful toys and good things to eat for all the children who lived on the other side of the mountain, but unfortunately, the engine broke down at the foot of the summit and asked for help from other passerby engines. Way too important to stop and lend a hand, both the shiny new passenger engine and the big strong freight engine went on their way, as did the rusty old engine that was just too tired to help. The little train that was filled with special treasures bound for boys and girls was left marooned on its tracks. That is, until a little blue engine came along.

The little blue engine was not as significant or as powerful as the passenger or freight engines or any other engines, for that matter. It was merely used for menial tasks, such as swapping trains down at the switch yard. As a matter of fact, the little blue engine had never even been over the mountain. But as the two engines talked that day, the heart of the little blue one went out to the one that was stranded and he decided he would give it a try. With much courage and confidence, he hooked up to the toy-filled railroad cars and slowly struggled up the incline, puffing out, "I think I can, I think I can, I think I can ..."

That story reminds me so much of a young shepherd boy in the Scriptures. His name was David and he was facing a mountain of his own, a giant Philistine who had been harassing the Israelites every morning before breakfast. One must admit, Goliath was one frightening sight to behold. Standing over nine feet tall, Goliath wore more than a whopping hundred and fifty pounds of armor. The spearhead on his spear shaft alone was a hefty twenty pounds. He was big, mean, loud, and everyone was afraid of him—everyone except, as Nazarene Evangelist Chuck Millhuff would say, "a red-faced farm boy!"

David had been sent by his father to the Valley of Elah to bring some cheese and other provisions for his brothers who served in the Israeli army. While there, he witnessed the taunts made by Goliath, a practice that had become the giant's daily morning routine. The fearsome Philistine would step out at daybreak to shame the Israelites and challenge any one of them to come out and engage with him in a match, but no one would accept his offer. No one had the courage to face the mammoth monster on the battlefield.

Could it be that's where you are today? What is *your* problem, *your* mountain, *your* giant? Is it financial? Finances, or the lack thereof, can cause an enormous amount of stress, make one sick, even destroy a marriage. The bills will continue to land in your mailbox whether or not there is money in the bank. The rent will still be due; the groceries still need to be bought, and clothes still must be purchased, regardless of how much the bank says you're worth. You're doing the best you can, but your best is not always enough, and all you're doing is getting farther behind and deeper in debt. Sometimes such a dilemma can push a person to commit the unthinkable and add upon the financial crisis a multitude of sins.

Could it be that your trouble is your job situation? Maybe you believe you deserve a promotion, you're wanting a new job, or perhaps you just need employment, period. When we moved to New Castle, Indiana in 2009, we were welcomed by abandoned railroad cars covered in graffiti and wrapped with vines, painful but constant reminders that the Chrysler plant had vacated the once thriving community and many hard, faithful workers were left unemployed. Before leaving Oklahoma, we even came across a TV documentary entitled, *The Trains That Go Nowhere.* We were somewhat shocked to learn that it was all about New Castle, Indiana, what was to be our new home! Many families of that community were greatly affected but so was the entire town. One by one, stores, restaurants, and businesses closed down, some leaving empty shells of buildings that still stand like those of a ghost town.

Other people struggle with family problems. There's trouble at school, a catastrophe at work, strained communication between parents and children, maybe even the lack of communication between husband and wife. Marriages fail, divorce takes place, homes are broken, families are separated. Whatever it is, there is a mountain that looms tall in your sights, one that seems to even grow larger at midnight. For our particular church in Nebraska, it was our assigned, yet unpaid budgets. I think David and Goliath can help us all. Notice a few things with me about *"the red-faced shepherd boy"* …

NOTICE DAVID'S POSITIVE ATTITUDE

A great Nazarene preacher, author, and evangelist, T.W. Willingham, called a lack of faith "the great handicap."[2] This was definitely not the case with young David. He didn't say that He *hoped* God would help him or that he *believed* God just might come through. The shepherd boy exclaimed of his Creator, "He will deliver me!" For David, there was no doubt about it. He had tremendous faith that his God would intervene.

Now, on the other hand, Saul, commander-in-chief of the Israeli army, clearly displayed a case of small thinking. He had emphatically told David, "You are not able to go against this Philistine to fight with him; for you are a youth, and he a man of war from his youth." (1 Samuel 17:33). The NIV has Saul saying, "you are only a boy." So while Saul says, "you can't," David says, "God can." While the king says, "you're not able," the shepherd boy says, "but He is able." A young lamb-sitter teaches us there is no room in Christianity for pessimism, smallness, and negative attitudes. There's just not a place for thimble-thinkers. That's why the Apostle Paul advised the Philippians to focus their thoughts on things that are just, pure, lovely, and of good report. (Philippians 4:8)

NOTICE DAVID'S PAST EXPERIENCE

A couple of ferocious animals are mentioned in the Bible—lions and bears. Common in Palestine during Bible times, Asiatic lions were similar to our African lions and are mentioned over one hundred thirty times in the Old Testament. As for bears, this incident in 1 Samuel 17 was probably a reference to a species of brown bear. More feared than lions, these vicious bears were stronger and even much more unpredictable. Unable to find berries during the lean winter months, these bears would raid the flocks and feast on tasty lambs. Although David was young, he had been in the pastures long enough to encounter the enemy. His faith for facing a giant was strengthened once he recalled, "The Lord, who saved me from the paw of the lion and from the paw of the bear, He will save me from the hand of this Philistine." (1 Samuel 17:37)

From the pulpit in that small Nazarene church, I reminded our good people of the mighty hand of God in days gone by. January 4, 1981 was a pledge Sunday to raise $5,000 to pay off the building to declare our church debt-free. From about fifty people (with a fourth of them being children), God helped us raise $6,050 in promises on that day! February 1, 1981, our "$5,000 Day," was a snowy Sunday morning but the weather didn't hinder us from raising $595 over our goal! On Easter Sunday morning in 1982, our church of forty attendees had an attendance of 102, winning the six-week spring Sunday School campaign for our zone! Over and over again, we witnessed God at work in our church, and we had no reason to doubt Him now.

Are you a little fearful of the future right now? There are moments when I find myself there, as well. Perhaps you and I need to look back and remember the times when God came through for us. We should recall each and every instance when we were backed against the wall, only to be gloriously delivered by the Lord Himself. We must recall when the lions and bears raided our own camps but God showed up with His powerful protection. We need to think again on both the days and nights that were so terribly dark until Jesus entered the inky blackness, saying, "I am the light of the world." Not long ago, I heard Dr. Jim Diehl preach a powerful revival sermon in Anderson, Indiana on God's ability to turn the curse into a blessing. That's the God we serve! He is the One Who's with us. Those times of victory will encourage us for whatever we face this day.

NOTICE DAVID'S POWERFUL GOD

The shepherd boy knew he was neither big enough nor strong enough to take on a veteran warrior who stood over nine feet tall. He was totally relying upon the God he served. We all know the outcome of the story for we learned it as a wee one in Sunday School. Saul's armor had been offered, but David, being unfamiliar with it, could not even walk in it—it swallowed him! David had to fight in his own armor, in his own way, with his own personal God-given talents and abilities. He couldn't be someone else nor act like or look like another. David could only be David.

Making a quick trek to the nearest brook, the shepherd boy reached into the babbling water and selected five smooth stones. He quickly returned to the battlefield, exchanged a few words with the frightening Philistine, and using his sling, David sank one of those rocks right smack dab in the middle of Goliath's forehead, a fatal shot. But this was not something David did. He was quick to give the glory to God: "The battle is the Lord's!" (1 Samuel 17:47)

The same God who delivered David from Goliath also delivered Daniel from a den of hungry lions, the three young Hebrews from a fiery furnace, blind Bartimaeus from a world of darkness, a boatload of disciples from a raging storm,

Lazarus from a cold tomb of death, and our church from a stressful lawsuit. He can deliver you from whatever has you presently entrapped. As a matter of fact, our Lord asks us for the opportunity to prove Himself in our lives: "Be still, and know that I am God." (Psalm 46:10)

By the way, I've heard some people cheapen David's faith by saying that, had he truly trusted God, he would not have picked up five stones, but only one. Well, over in 2 Kings, we read that Goliath had four sons, all big boys, as well. I think David picked up a stone to kill the giant and thought, *I heard that he has four boys who look just like him. I might as well get four more rocks and take care of them, too!* David finally caught up with the other four members of the Goliath family and ridded the world of them as well. (2 Samuel 21:22) The way I see it, grabbing four stones did nothing but strengthen David's unswerving trust in a mighty big God.

Watty Piper tells us that the little blue engine hooked up with the cars that carried the toys and he started up the mountain toward uncharted territory. He began to say to himself, "I think I can, I think I can, I think I can ..." Finally topping the summit, the train started its descent on the other side, saying, "I thought I could, I thought I could, I thought I could ..." That little story so inspired me that I stood before my people the next Sunday and preached a sermon entitled, "The Little Engine That Could!" At the close of the service, we received a special offering and raised enough money to overpay the budgets we owed for that assembly year! Of course, all the glory goes to God.

You and I can learn today from a little engine with a big attitude. As we face our mountain, as we stand at the brink of our river, as we stare at that obstacle that stands in our way, we must recall times when God has worked in our past and muster up the faith to believe He can do it again.

CHAPTER FIVE

FAITH THAT MOVES MOUNTAINS

… if you had faith even as small as a mustard seed, you could say to this mountain, "Move from here to there," and it would move.Nothing would be impossible."

(Matthew 17:20, NLT)

Rev. R.C. Goddard was my Grandfather, a circuit-riding Nazarene preacher who alternated his ministry among three small Methodist churches on Sundays. By the time I was born, he had retired from his preaching circuit as well as from his full time job as a U.S. postal worker. He never stopped working, however, for he preached whenever and wherever he had the opportunity, and he worked on Gravely tractors in his spare time. And oh yes, he was also a farmer.

He had a small farm just behind his house on Tilson Road in Decatur, Georgia, just outside Atlanta.

One thing that impressed me about "Paw Paw Goddard," was that he was a man of great faith. Though I was too small to understand what was wrong, I remember one night when my Mom seemed to be very ill. I recall standing by her bed in the darkened room and seeing her, lighted only by the nightlight plugged into the wall outlet. My mother was crying and I heard her ask my Dad if he would call his father. I still remember the sound of the low rumblings of my Granddad's old black Ford pickup truck with the homemade wooden front bumper as he drove up in front of our house. My Dad invited him in, and he went straight to my Mom, laying his hands on her shoulders and praying the glory down. Trying to process all that was happening, I was sure of only one thing: My Granddad evidently had a kind of faith in which others strongly believed.

Now you must understand that my Granddad was typically very calm and easy-going, seldom aggravated. There was one thing, however, that got him agitated. Just behind his home was a big hill that separated his house from his farm. Every morning he got into his truck and drove the little path that led him around the hill in order to get to his field for the day. Every afternoon when it was time to end the day, he made that same trip back, winding around that huge hill of dirt and grass. With each and every passing year, that hill became more and more of a nuisance.

When my brother and I were young boys, we lived about thirty minutes away from our grandparents and occasionally, our Mom and Dad would take us over for a visit. I can still remember how, upon our arrival, the adults would go into the house and Harold and I would head for the hill. It was a huge mount, perhaps a couple of stories high, and we would immediately begin our ascent. Once we were on top of the hill, we thought we were on top of the world. We would run across to the other side which only took a minute, and look out over our grandfather's farm. I still remember watching as our Grandfather drove his truck along the road below us, unaware of our hovering presence.

Now, that mound behind my Grandparents' dwelling was probably best described as a *"hill,"* but to my Granddad, it was a *"mountain."* It was definitely in his way and he increasingly grew more tired day by day of driving around that hill to get to his crops. As a matter of fact, I remember Wednesday night testimony time at Atlanta First Church of the Nazarene when Paw Paw Goddard would stand to his feet and testify about his *"mountain."* He told how he had read in the Bible that Jesus said if you have enough faith, you can tell a mountain to move and it will. (Matthew 17:20) He therefore claimed that verse as his own and told everyone that God was going to move the *"mountain"* that loomed outside his kitchen door!

This went on week after week, Wednesday after Wednesday. Atlanta Nazarenes smiled when Rev. R.C. Goddard stood to testify. I remember how some would snicker. They knew he was going to tell about his *"mountain"* and God's promise to answer prayer. They also knew that, though they found it a bit humorous, they realized my Granddad really did possess a powerful faith in God, the God Who can move mighty mountains. As he would testify, they all nodded in agreement and assured him of their prayerful support.

I cannot help but wonder, however, if Rev. R.C. Goddard was really the only one exercising any amount of genuine faith among those believers.

Sandie and I recently attended a high school basketball game in New Castle, Indiana—basketball country, U.S.A. One Trojans fan sitting a few rows down and in front of us was sporting a t-shirt with the words across his back in bold letters: "BELIEVE IN THE IMPOSSIBLE." Though it could sound spiritual, other information on his shirt led one to believe his slogan was referring to basketball. My Grandfather did exactly what that shirt advised, except it was all about his horrendous hill. He actually believed God was going to move his *"mountain."*

I wonder if this story has struck a chord with you. Is there some sort of *"mountain"* in your life? Perhaps you are a pastor and your church seems to be at a standstill. You need to see new people come in, you need to see some growth in your congregation, you need a spiritual breakthrough, a real revival, but it's just not happening. Maybe you're a lay-person and you want to see the Sunday School class you teach really take off and grow. Or perhaps you've received bad news from your physician. You may have even heard the word *cancer* and you are not sure what the future holds. Could it be that you are tempted to believe God for a mighty miracle but you are surrounded by so many who just cannot agree with your spirit?

It could be that you are a husband or a wife and your marriage is on the rocks. There doesn't seem to be any other answer for you and your spouse than separation or even divorce. Or it might be that you have a son or daughter who is spiritually lost and you've been faithfully praying for his or her salvation for a long, long time. Perhaps you're like the desperate Amish father who had erected a big sign that I saw in his cornfield near the road just outside Shipshewana, Indiana, "SON, WILL YOU PLEASE COME BACK TO JESUS?" You may even fast meals on a regular basis for the salvation of your loved one. Each of these is an obstacle, a *"mountain,"* that stands tall in your way. All you seem to be able to do is stand at the foot of your mount and stare with a hopeless look on your face, day after day, night after night. Once you're able to tune all the other voices out and listen closely, perhaps you will hear God saying to you what he said to Moses and the Israelites at Mount Horeb: "You have stayed long enough at this mountain." (Deuteronomy 1:6)

It was by such a peak of concern that a father stood with his very sick boy. Jesus and a few of His faithful followers had just come down from an amazing experience on a mountain when He was met by the distraught Dad. The man exclaimed, "Lord, have mercy on my son, for he is an epileptic and he suffers terribly." (Matthew 17:15) The literal meaning is that the boy was "moonstruck." Some versions call him a "lunatic." The Living Bible translates, "he is mentally deranged and in great trouble," and the New International Version simply says, "He has seizures and is suffering greatly." In his gospel, Mark explains how the boy suddenly collapses, foams at the mouth, gnashes his teeth, and becomes rigid. (Mark 9:18) This had to be a frightening experience for both father and son. Luke adds that the boy is an only child. (Luke 9:38) This boy obviously has a real problem, one that has become a huge *"mountain"* in his life as well as in that of his father and family. But good news: At least the disciples of Jesus were nearby! ...

Word on the street was that these guys had been empowered. (Matthew 10:1) They didn't look like much but they had become the talk of the town. Rumors circulating said they could do anything. (Matthew 10:8) Surely, if anyone could help it would be these close companions of the Miracle Man, Jesus of Nazareth! This predicament would be nothing for these guys! However, the frantic father said of his son to Jesus, "I brought him to your disciples, but they could not cure him." (Matthew 17:16) This must have been so frustrating, not to mention embarrassing, to the disciples of Christ, just as it is frustrating to you and me when our prayer doesn't seem to get answered and the mountain remains like an elephant in the room.

These apostles may have appeared to the general public as a ragtag bunch of believers, but this situation was precisely the reason they had been trained. Empowered and sent out by Jesus Himself, their task had been to take care of these kinds of issues. They knew where to stand, how to pray, what to say, how to hold their mouths! But this time nothing clicked and it was frustrating—frustrating and embarrassing.

Not too long ago, I officiated a beautiful wedding at Salyer Lake in Southwest Oklahoma. It was a gorgeous Saturday afternoon of Easter weekend and as I was waiting just outside a gazebo for the ceremony to begin, I noticed a little boy in his suit and tie, playing with a colorful plastic egg. I asked him what was in the egg and he replied, "My medicine and pills!" My heart sank, for I assumed he must have some kind of serious illness. I asked if the pills made him feel better and he very seriously said, "Sometimes." I then watched as he carefully opened the egg to expose its contents—jelly beans! Red ones, yellow ones, white ones, and licorice—jelly beans! I said, "Those pills look like jelly beans to me!" The little boy answered, "Yeah, sometimes they look like jelly beans!"

Sometimes we believers take on an appearance, as well. We may look like we're so Christlike, as if we have it all together, spiritually. People may see us on some kind of pedestal, walking so very closely with our Creator. Some may even use us as some sort of measuring stick to describe how Christianity is supposed to look. We appear to have an answer for everything, but instead, we find ourselves right smack dab in the middle of life; we find that we are, in reality, frustrated followers of the Lord Jesus!

Those disciples stood and watched as Jesus, the Master, took over …

> "Jesus answered, 'You faithless and perverse generation, how much longer must I be with you? How much longer must I put up with you? Bring him here to me.' And Jesus rebuked the demon, and it came out of him, and the boy was cured instantly. Then the disciples came to Jesus privately and said, 'Why could we not cast it out?' He said to them, 'Because of your little faith. For truly I tell you, if you have faith the size of a mustard seed, you will say to this mountain, "Move from here to there," and it will move; and nothing will be impossible for you.'" (Matthew 17:17-20)

One can almost hear the anger in the words of Christ. Why was He so put-out, so disappointed with His selected few? What was it about His boys that angered Him so? It is because Jesus had expected them to get the job done! He had fully anticipated His trained disciples would heal the sick lad. Jesus had fully assumed His faithful followers would unleash the power of Almighty God! Our Lord completely trusted those guys to make a difference at the foot of the mountain that day in the lives of a boy and his Dad. What was their predicament? What was the boy's problem?

Even though the Gospel writers allude to some kind of existing devil, the boy's dilemma was far from demon-possession. I checked several major commentaries (William Barclay, Adam Clark, Matthew Henry, Jamieson, Fausset, and Brown, Keil and Delitzsch, Wycliffe, Barnes' Notes, and Warren Wiersbe) and they all downplay demonology in this story. Though an evil spirit may have been involved, if we focus on that, we will miss the entire point of the pericope. This is not an account of demon-possession, but rather a sad look at a serious lack of faith. The Greek word in verse 20 literally means *littleness of faith*. There was a lack of confidence from the boy's father but also a mistrust among the disciples. As Wiersbe put it: "The main lesson of this miracle is the power of faith to overcome the enemy."[1]

The Living Bible translates Mark's descriptive account: "Then the demon screamed terribly and convulsed the boy again and left him; and the boy lay there limp and motionless, to all appearance dead. A murmur ran through the crowd— "He is dead." (Mark 9:26, TLB) Don't you love the murmurings?

Just before bitter waters were made sweet in the wilderness, the Bible says, "the people murmured against Moses …" (Exodus 15:24, KJV) Just prior to a chief tax collector's life being forever changed, Luke tells us of the people of Jericho, "And when they saw it, they all murmured …" (Luke 19:7, KJV) In the Book of Acts we read about the growth of the church, how the number of converts was multiplying across the land. As God was pouring out His Spirit upon His church and revival was on, we read the astonishing words, "there arose a murmuring." (Acts 6:1)

It's no different with us. When the mighty hand of God moves in our lives, it is usually followed by negative, discouraging "murmurings" … God heals someone of a dreaded disease like cancer! *I'm just afraid it might come back!* … God miraculously opens a door for the purchase of a new home! *I just hope we can make the payments!* … God blesses a church financially, providing for the month's needs! *But what will we do next month?* … God begins to bring a brand new thing! *But that's not the way we've done it before!*

Rev. R.C. Goddard kept reading the Scriptures about mountain-moving faith which only strengthened his own trust in His Creator and Savior. He continued to pray specifically for God to move his *"mountain,"* a sincere request he made without fail each and every day, especially each morning and afternoon as he drove to and from his field. He never gave up believing God for a miracle and he kept testifying in the midweek services about what his powerful and able God was going to do. He genuinely believed in his heart that God was going to answer his prayer in a miraculous way. Prayer is a must for every child of God.

In his inspiring book, *The Hour That Changes the World*, Dick Eastman explains:

> *God will bless Elijah and send rain on Israel, but Elijah must pray for it. If the chosen nation is to prosper, Samuel must plead for it. If the Jews are to be delivered, Daniel must intercede. God will bless Paul, and the nations shall be converted through him, but Paul must pray. Pray he did without ceasing; his epistles show that he expected nothing except by asking for it.*[2]

James tells us that many believers never experience a miracle; they never see an answer to prayer, simply because they never pray. (James 4:2) Prayerlessness is certainly something of which Rev. R.C. Goddard could never be accused. He had learned to become a man of prayer.

Early one morning in Decatur, Georgia, just as the birds began to sing and my Granddad had finished breakfast, he was startled by a knock at the front door. Unaccustomed to visitors at such an early hour, he went to the door and walked out onto the porch where he found two or three men wearing coveralls and brightly-colored hard hats. After introducing themselves, they got straight to the point. They asked my grandfather if he owned his home and the property it sat on. He acknowledged that he did. Carefully choosing their words, they explained how they were working on a construction site a mile or so up the road and were badly in need of fill dirt. Every day as they drove up and down Tilson Road, they couldn't help but notice the big hill that stood tall behind my grandfather's house. They were prepared to offer him a reasonable sum of money to purchase that hill in order to use the soil on their project.

I would have loved to have been there to see the look on my Granddad's face. I don't think it was a look of surprise, however, but rather, a look of satisfaction, an appearance of assurance. Rev. Goddard had been praying faithfully for God to move his hill and now his plea was being handled. The deal was made, the papers were signed, and a few days later the workers returned with huge excavation equipment. They filled dump truck after dump truck with dirt until my grandparents' backyard had been completely leveled. Those helmet-clad construction workers, no, my Granddad's gracious God had literally moved that *"mountain!"*

The following Wednesday night church was on at old Atlanta First Church and it was soon testimony time. I'm sure there were probably some wonderful praises from Dora Jones or Brother Chilton or Sister Goodson, but then Rev. R.C. Goddard stood to his feet. No doubt, a few people had grown weary of his plight and his plea, but this time was different. This time as he told his story with a twinkle in his eye, he was able to praise God for having moved his *"mountain!"* My grandfather was a short man, only reaching my shoulder when I was a teenager, but when I preached his funeral as a freshman in college, he was ten feet tall, all because he had possessed a faith that could move mountains. Perhaps today is the day when God will move yours.

CHAPTER SIX

WHAT is FAITH?

Now faith is the substance of things hoped for,
the evidence of things not seen.
(Hebrews 11:1, NKJV)

The Atlanta Hartsfield-Jackson International Airport is no small place. Today as I write, I have set-up shop at Gate B31 in that very setting. Everywhere I look, there are scores of people, no, hundreds of folk, no, there are thousands of human beings, maybe millions, coming and going in all directions. Most have a serious look in their eye. Most appear to be on a mission. Many look stressed to the max. My wife and I just got off the train that connects the concourses, a subway that was packed with passengers from door-to-door like sardines in a can. Once we had disembarked and began our attempt to move along with the mob, I commented to Sandie, "I think a third of Atlanta is in this airport!"

That statement was not meant to be derogatory—it was just a fact. I love Atlanta, Georgia. It's my home. It's where I was born. It's where I grew up. It's where I attended high school. It's the location of so many fond memories. It's where my parents are buried. It's where I met my wife. It's where I once turned down an unbelievable job offer of relocating to Jacksonville, Florida with Sears to have my own art department, but I told my supervisor, "I'll never leave Atlanta!" It's the place I miss the most. I have now been gone for more decades than I lived there and the city essentially grew without me. However, contrary to popular opinion, I have always enjoyed coming back through, even if it's only for an airport layover. It just dawned on me that everyone in this part of the airport is flying to or from someplace, for we are all past security. That means thousands of people in this vicinity are exercising faith this very afternoon.

Exercising faith? Sure. For one thing, they are showing faith in a pilot they don't even know. Since I love helicopters even more than jets and planes, I once saw a sign on an interstate in Orlando advertising helicopter rides and I promptly took the first exit. I parked the car, and leaving my family, I got out and ran inside the building to get the scoop. The prices were a bit steep for me but I do admit I was seriously considering a chopper tour around the town—until I saw the pilot. He had just landed his whirlybird upon the circle painted on the pavement just outside the building and was walking our way. His hair was disheveled above his red face. His shirt tail was out of his pants but only on one side. And, oh, he appear-ed to be very much inebriated! He almost staggered toward the office and asked if he could help us, but I quickly responded that he could not. As much as I have an infatuation for helicopters and as much as I had enjoyed previous flights in the past, I just had no confidence in this particular chopper chauffeur. According to Dr. Billy Graham, that's exactly what faith is all about: "Faith is complete confidence."[1]

Many times, if not most, we board an aircraft at an airport and we don't even get a glimpse of who's in the cockpit. That means there are lots of people at this airport today who are placing their faith in someone about whom they know nothing. They don't know how much sleep she got the night before. They have no way of knowing whether or not he had drinks at the sky bar within the last few hours. Unsuspect-ing passengers board a jet, find their seat, and relax with music piped through ear buds until they reach their destina-tion. Faith.

They also have faith in an aircraft. I would guess that most people don't know the difference between a B52 and a C130, yet they board with a blind trust that this soon-to-be-airborne tube of steel is going to get them safely from point A to point B. We don't know the date of its last service or repair or how new the engines may be. We have no way of knowing if all the screws are screwed down and all the bolts are bolted tight. Unlike earlier years, we board from the jet way directly onto the aircraft so we don't even have an opportunity to kick the tires for good luck. And yet we get buckled into our seats and soar high above the clouds while we snooze or solve Sudoku puzzles or carry on a conversation with our neighbor as if all is well in River City.

Not only do people put their faith in a pilot and an aircraft, but they also put their trust in the elements. I have taken off and landed in some terrible thunderstorms. As I often read books on flights, I always use a red razor point pen to underline important thoughts and write notes in the margins. My wife thinks I should underline the unimportant lines because it would save ink. One can tell how bumpy my flight was by how curvy my underlines are. I once boarded a jet in Dallas and, shortly after I was seated, watched out the window as a mechanic walked back and forth across the wing, carefully examining every inch of that appendage. We were soon enlightened by the pilot: Prior to that plane's landing, that particular aircraft had been struck by lightning, blistering the skin on the wing. The man in coveralls was making sure the damage was not severe. Yet all we think about is getting above the storm as quickly as possible and all will be fine.

Dr. John Bowling, President of Olivet Nazarene University in Kankakee, Illinois, says not only is faith essential to our Christian lives, but it is extremely important where it is rested. Though we may put our faith in people or things such as pilots and planes, the One upon Whom we absolutely must rely is the One Who created us. Dr. Bowling writes, "It is not enough just to believe or just to have faith. We must be careful where we rest our faith." He adds in his next paragraph, "There is only one sufficient place in which to let your faith rest, and that is in God."[2]

According to the writer to the Hebrews, "Now faith is being sure of what we hope for and certain of what we do not see." (Hebrews 11:1) What, exactly, does that mean? I think it covers at least three things.

FAITH IS BELIEVING

Believing begins with hope for something that I cannot see because it does not yet exist, but I sure do long for it to become reality. I just believe with everything within me that it is actually going to come to pass. The Message says of faith: "It's our handle on what we can't see." (Hebrews 11:1, MSG)

Young and still newlyweds, we had moved to our second pastorate in Columbus, Nebraska. Wanting to keep ourselves in shape, we visited the local Nautilus, a health club for exercise and body building. The young, ambitious instructor took us on a quick tour, then signed us up as card-carrying members. As we filled out paperwork and responded to personal questions, he first asked me, "What is your goal?" At that very moment, a body builder walked by in a Speedo, muscles rippling all over, sure to be "Mr. Some City" in championship competition, if he wasn't already. I pointed to the blond adonis and said, "I want to look like him!" That brought a roar of laughter (except from the solemn instructor) because we all knew that such a metamorphosis was highly impossible and that I was only kidding. But faith is believing the impossible. Faith is a man believing it's going to rain, though it never had throughout the history of time, and even going so far as to spend over a hundred and twenty years building a huge boat to save the animals. Faith is a man believing even in his old age that not only was his wife going to conceive and give him a son but that he would eventually become the father of many nations. As a matter of fact, a sign on the wall of that Nebraska health club read, *Age has nothing to do with it, desire does.*

Sandie and I recently boarded an eastbound jet in Orange County, California. Sitting on the tarmac and staring out the window as our bags were loaded onto the plane, my wife noticed one tiny cloud in a beautiful, sunny southern California sky. She turned to me and said with a smile that it was about the size of a man's hand! I knew she was referring to one of our favorite Old Testament stories. After a three-and-half year drought, Elijah the Tishbite told King Ahab that he had better hurry back to town because there was coming a downpour! As the prophet knelt and prayed, he repeatedly sent his servant to check the sky for signs of precipitation. Going back and forth eight times, the servant finally said, "a little cloud no bigger than a person's hand is rising out of the sea." (1 Kings 18:44, NRSV) That's all Elijah needed to know! He suddenly sprang into action, heading for Jezreel. The clouds rolled in black and heavy and soon there was a thunderous rainstorm. In the South, we would have said, "The bottom fell out!" The Lord came upon Elijah, who girded up his loins and ran into the city, passing the king's speeding chariot in the process! That's faith.

Now the song says *"It never rains in sunny southern California,"* but wouldn't you know it, with a small cloud in the sky, we took off from the west coast only to encounter rain on the way to Phoenix. We left Phoenix for Indianapolis but landed a half hour late because the pilot told us he took us way around a huge storm that had covered much of the country! By the time we drove an hour home, the storm caught up with us, producing rain, thunder, and even some circulation. Our day had begun with a tiny fist-sized cloud that most people hadn't even noticed. Faith is believing.

FAITH IS TRUSTING

I love to read anything that focuses on faith. Together, three authors, Wes

Harmon, Vicki Hesterman, and Dean Nelson, wrote such a chapter in the book, *I Believe,* edited by Everett Leadingham. Referring to spectacular events of the Old Testament, they wrote, "By faith, the waters of the Red Sea parted to reveal dry land. And by faith, the solid walls of Jericho came crashing down. Yet for many people today, the big question is: Can I make it through another day?"[3]

So how does one exercise faith in tomorrow? When someone has just lost their job and they have bills to pay and mouths to feed—how is he going to survive? When the news from the doctor was anything but encouraging and her whole life seems to be crashing in around her, how will she ever cope? As the family wearing black clothes and dark glasses hesitantly walks away from the graveside, leaving their loved one forever in a cold, black hole in the ground, how can they face another day of life without their mom or dad or son or daughter? I think the only answer we have is that we need to simply trust Jesus. With a stern stance of seriousness, our Lord said, "Come unto Me, all ye that labor and are heavy laden, and I will give you rest." (Matthew 11:28, KJV) The Message translates, "Are you tired? Worn out? Burned out on religion? Come to me. Get away with me and you'll recover your life. I'll show you how to take a real rest." Sounds like a vacation for which many of us need to sign-up! It's simply trusting Jesus.

I think most of us want to trust Him and we know that He expects that from us, but do we really do it? I don't know what its practice is today, but years ago, the Will Rogers Airport in Oklahoma City didn't open until 5 a.m. Knowing you are expected there two hours early, I was a good passenger and showed up at 4 a.m. for my 6 a.m. flight. After spending some time on a bench, they finally opened the counter so I could check-in. I made my way toward security, quickly realizing I would be the first passenger through TSA for the day.

Having successfully made it through the screening device, I waited patiently by the conveyor belt and rollers to retrieve my carry-ons. The young TSA agent was cheerful for 5 o'clock in the morning. She pulled my laptop case off the belt and asked me to follow her to a little table where she began to swab my bag with some kind of solution. As she worked, she asked, "Are you a Nazarene pastor?" "Yes, I am," I replied in surprise. "I'm pastor at Yukon First Church." Wondering how she had recognized me, I asked, "Are you a Nazarene?" "Yes, I am," she answered, as she dutifully continued to swab my bag. "I attend Oklahoma City First Church." I mentioned that I really liked her pastor and how I had been in her church on a few occasions, no doubt how she knew me. I watched as she stayed busy at her job, devotedly swabbing almost every inch of my computer bag. I finally asked her, "So what are you looking for?" Without hesitation, she responded, "Explosives!" We had identified one another, engaged in small-talk, even understood that we were both of the same religious persuasion—brother and sister in Christ as well as Nazarenedom, but all of a sudden I didn't feel very trusted by this faithful TSA agent.

Gordon E. and Phyllisee Foust Jackson wrote a very interesting book, *Pathways to Faith*. They had interviewed 150 laypeople (an equal amount of men and women) and 60 religious professionals (36 pastors and 24 seminary professors). These people represented United Methodists, Presbyterians, Baptists, Lutherans, and United Church of Christ from all across the United States. They were all questioned about faith and the authors concluded: "Faith as trust is an attitudinal response to the material of life."[4]

FAITH IS PROCEEDING

Could it be that faith really isn't faith until it is exercised, put into action? When one truly demonstrates faith, he or she scoots out on that little limb, trusting God in the breeze. Faith means proceeding ahead because of what we strongly believe.

In *My Soul Purpose*, Richard Parrott suggests that faith enriches our daily lives, strengthens our most important relationships, and advances us toward our God-given potential. He elaborates: "There is faith in what God has done for you on the Cross of Christ. There is faith in what God does in you through the Spirit of Christ. And there is faith in cooperating with the Father's will to bring your true and best in Christ to the challenges of life."[5]

So, having said all that, what is faith? The word *"faith"* is an English word for a Greek noun, *pistis*, formed from the verb in the phrase *"believe into"* (*pisteuo*). It carries the idea of trustful commitment and reliance better than merely *"belief."* According to J.I. Packer, "Whereas 'belief' suggests bare opinion, 'faith,' whether in a car, a patent medicine, a protégé, a doctor, a marriage partner, or what have you, is a matter of treating the person or thing as trustworthy and committing yourself accordingly. The same is true of faith in God, and in a more far-reaching way."[6]

The offer and demand of the object is what determines what a faith-commitment involves. For example, I exercise faith in my car by relying on it to get me to my destination. You show faith in your physician by following doctor's orders and doing all that he or she prescribes. In much the same way, we demonstrate faith in God by surrendering to Him and living by His Holy Word.

Max Lucado gives a great illustration of this in his book, *3:16.* Lucado tells of Bible translators in the New Hebrides islands who were struggling over finding the most appropriate verb for the English word, *"believe."* Translator John Paton was out hunting with a tribesman when they bagged a large deer and had to carry the carcass on a pole up a steep mountain path. Once they arrived home, their load was dropped and they both collapsed into chairs on the porch. That's when the native had exclaimed in his native tongue, "It is good to stretch yourself out and rest!" That was it! That's the word! Paton grabbed paper and pen and wrote it down. Faith in Christ means we are going to stretch ourselves out on Him and rest.[7]

Preconceived ideas and prejudices create problems for us all, and many people have deep doubts about elements of the biblical message. How do these doubts relate to faith?

Exercising faith is certainly the intent of the Christian but even when we are doing our best to trust God, there's still a dab of doubt somewhere in the back of our thoughts. The father of the sick boy put it this way: "I do believe; help me overcome my unbelief!" (Mark 9:24, NIV) Packer defines *doubt* as "a state of divided mind."[8] James referred to this as "double-mindedness," (James 1:4-8) and his solution is to "Draw near to God, and he will draw near to you. Cleanse your hands, you sinners, and purify your hearts, you double-minded." (James 4:8, NRSV) In other words, one should be sanctified wholly in order to be forgiven of the things we do (*clean hands*) and to be free from carnality (*a pure heart*). Only then can we truly deal with the doubts.

So back to the original question, "What is faith?" Well, it's not quite the little Sunday School boy's definition: "believing something that isn't so." I like Fletcher Spruce's definition better: Faith is "believing that God will do what He said He would do."[9] Yes, we can absolutely put our complete confidence in God and trust Him to come through. We can stand upon His promises and know that He is not going to let us down.

Where do we fit into the equation? Even when everything and everyone is against us, we can still believe God for the impossible. We can overcome that tad of doubt and draw from a bottomless sea of tremendous belief in a prayer-answering God. The question is, do you have such great faith?

CHAPTER SEVEN

BELIEVING is SEEING

*Then the Lord opened the eyes of the young man,
and he saw. And behold, the mountain was full
of horses and chariots of fire
all around Elisha.*
(2 Kings 6:17 NKJV)

When our son, Tommy, was three or four years old, his Mom would ask him who had been into the chips or who had failed to put the TV remote back in its proper place, and so often, the little one was not to blame. It was usually about then that I arrived on the scene, took note of what was going on, and admitted my role in the crime. It was also then that Tommy, with that little pointing, accusing finger, would say to me, "So YOU'RE the crook!" Those incriminating words would become a household phrase in the Goddard home for years to come.

Syria and Israel were at war but it appeared that every time the king of Syria made a move, Israel was already amazingly aware. The Syrian king consulted with his servant, wondering how the king of Israel always seemed to know his plans before they were carried out. The answer, in Tommy's words: "Elisha was the crook!" The prophet Elisha would clue his king in on everything the Syrians were planning, thereby keeping Israel a step or two ahead of the enemy. I like the way the Syrian servant put it to his king, "Elisha, the prophet who is in Israel, tells the king of Israel the words that you speak in your bedroom." (2 Kings 6:12)

Understanding the prophet was in Dothan (not Alabama), the king of Syria sent a great army with horses and chariots during the night to capture Elisha. The next morning his servant went outside the cottage and was alarmed to see that the whole city was surrounded by the enemy army. Running back inside in a panic, the servant exclaims to Elisha, "What shall we do?" (2 Kings 6:15)

Is that a picture of you? Do you ever panic in situations, wringing your hands in despair, and wondering what in the world your actions might be? Perhaps the responsibility lies on your shoulders and yours alone, and you must make some tough decisions that will affect the lives of others. What is your decision? What will you ever do?

Indianapolis TV meteorologists were calling it "the snowpocalypse of 2014." Only a few days after the new year had begun, it started with over eleven inches of the white stuff and temperatures of -12°. Of course, every flake of that predicted snow was to fall all night Saturday and into Sunday. Most of the churches in New Castle, Indiana, had already cancelled for Sunday on Saturday evening, but the governor of Indiana had not yet issued an orange alert to allow only essential cars on the roads. Still under a yellow alert, we were waiting in concerned anticipation for the big blizzard of the decade. I texted a few board members Saturday night to seek advice about our services and their opinions were split. Some said to cancel while others said to wait until morning. What should I do? Do I put my faith in the weather man or in the Weather-maker?

Sunday morning came and I hurried to the window to peek outside. It was 6:30 a.m., the street was clear, and contrary to the forecast, no new snow had fallen. I began texting back and forth with a police officer in our church who was working a twelve-hour shift on dispatch, fielding 911 calls. He gave me all the information available from the local news, the National Weather Service, and the radar that he monitored. I also was texting board members. Seeing no reason to cancel, I took a shower and got dressed. I sat around the house in my suit, wanting to make a decision by 8 a.m. so my administrative assistant could make a one-call (an automated telephone message) to our congregation.

Did I feel pressured? Yes, most definitely. Did I feel overwhelmed with the responsibility of 300+ people? Yes, I sure did. Now, understand that I realized all of those folks would not get out on a day like this, even to hear my sermon. I would guess a hundred or so might show up. But as my wife and I talked, it was clear that many of the ones who would venture out would be the ones who shouldn't—the older ones, the faithful saints of the church, the ones who didn't dare miss a Sunday morning service if the doors were open. After lots of prayer and contemplation that included going back and forth in my thinking, I finally reached a decision. We needed to protect the safety of our people, and I texted Sheri to put out a message that church was closed for the day. Getting to church would not be a problem but getting home might be, since the snow was now predicted for mid-morning. By 10 a.m. white stuff was falling and it for sure wasn't manna. I began to receive texts and Facebook messages affirming I had done the right thing.

The prophet's servant was there in the same place, not in the "snowpocalypse," but in the position of panic, not knowing what to do. There were only two of them and they were clearly surrounded on all sides by rival soldiers. What would be the wise advice of the prophet of God? Elisha answered, "Do not be afraid, for there are more with us than there are with them." (2 Kings 6:16) The Scripture goes on to say, "Then Elisha prayed: 'O Lord, please open his eyes that he may see.' So the Lord opened the eyes of the servant, and he saw; the mountain was full of horses and chariots of fire all around Elisha." (2 Kings 6:17) Wow! What a story! That's exactly what we need, for our eyes to be opened in order that we might see what God sees. "Open our eyes, Lord" is more than a song. It should be the prayer of every born again child of God.

Shortly after our plane's takeoff, the little boy behind us blurted out: "I can see the whole world!" Some people think they can see a long way, but God wants us to see even further. He wants us to see into another realm, that of faith. Jim Cymbala defines faith as "total dependence upon God that becomes supernatural in its working. People with faith develop a second kind of sight; they see God, right beside them."[1] What does that mean? Here's what I believe it means…

When I was studying to be a minister, my pastor and mentor, Dr. Jim Diehl, taught me that, as a pastor, I must be able to see with my *"mind's eye."* I often go to the church early on weekday mornings when no one is around. The first thing I see as I get out of my car is the parking lot. Although my vehicle is the only one there, with my *"mind's eye,"* I can see the parking lot filled to capacity with cars and SUVs and what my father-in-law used to call, "pick-'em-up trucks." Not only are they parked in the lot, but they also line the street and many are on the grass! I go inside to the sanctuary and, from the pulpit, I look out at empty pews, but with my *"mind's eye,"* I see every single seat taken, even in the overflow! Some children are having to sit on laps. The ushers are bringing out folding chairs and setting them up in the aisles! The platform is filled with various musical instruments to make up a huge orchestra! The choir loft is completely full of singers of all ages and they are singing for the glory of God! Worship is on with a sanctuary filled to the brim with God-loving believers.

I listen in that empty auditorium and all I hear are the occasional "pops" and "cracks" of a vacated church building, but with my *"mind's ear,"* I hear the thunderous voices of a mammoth choir, the beautiful music of talented instrumentalists, and the welcomed sounds of the glorious shouts of our people. The singing and music can be heard outside the building to the point of neighbors calling us the "Noisarenes," as they did at Los Angeles First Church of the Nazarene back in the early 1900s. Glancing toward the bare altars, I see with my *"mind's eye,"* people kneeling and praying from one end of the altars to the other! They hang over our mourner's benches, some praising God, others begging for forgiveness. Many believers are consecrating their entire beings to become sanctified through and through. What a glorious sight—lives being radically changed by the unmistakable presence and power of Almighty God! There is excitement in the air! There is anticipation in the hearts of people. Everyone soon leaves but each can hardly wait to bring their unchurched friends and family members the next Sunday! That's what I have learned to *"see"* when I stare at my empty parking lot, vacant sanctuary, and barren altars.

How can I see all that on a weekday morning when the place is abandoned? It's because of faith. It's visualizing with the eyes of my mind, my mind that believes God can do anything. The New International Version of the Bible translates Hebrews 11:1 this way: "Now faith is being sure of what we hope for and certain of what we do not see."

Our church recently had a "Neighborhood Night," a time when we intentionally invite our community to come to our church on a Sunday afternoon/evening. We had a live DJ playing music in the parking lot. The kids played games, had their faces painted, and enjoyed a bounce house. Classic cars were on display and admired by young and old. Our parish nurse was at a table doing complimentary blood pressure checks, resulting in one lady being sent to the hospital, perhaps saving her from future trouble. Our men were grilling free hamburgers and hot dogs while the local shaved ice trailer was parked on the side where everyone could find their favorite flavor at no charge. It was a great time for all.

One table set up in our parking lot was a "Prayer Station." Pastors Jim and Woody sat there behind a sign that simply asked, "Can we pray with you?" Prayer request forms were filled out and dropped into a prayer box, like the one from the little girl who scribbled out her simple request, "Daddy." Rachel from across the street had only been in our church on Easter Sunday. Wandering through the various tables and stations, she found our prayer booth. After filling out a prayer request form, she told the ministers of the physical need of her daughter. They prayed with Rachel.

A couple of weeks passed and we were holding Vacation Bible School during the evenings. As Sandie and I were heading to our car on a Wednesday night after VBS, Rachel from across the street got our attention with waving arms. She had crossed the road and was walking toward us at the other end of the parking lot so we met her halfway. She wanted to tell us that on the day after our men had prayed with her, her daughter was completely healed! She said her girl was back to herself again. She also said, "This has restored my faith in God," adding that she would be in church on Sunday.

She kept her word and was, in fact, in our Sunday morning worship service. She soon found a Sunday School class and our Wednesday night midweek service. Rachel boarded our church bus aimed toward our annual district camp meeting and there she was gloriously saved at an altar of prayer. A few months later, she attended the pastor's class that my wife and I teach and she became a member of our church. She attends church faithfully and is even an occasional member of our worship team. The "Rachels" continue to come as God continues to bless. These "Rachels" are the ones a pastor must see with his or her *"mind's eye."* With that kind of *"sight"* in mind, a minister is able to encourage, inspire, and lead a congregation.

In *Vertical Church,* James MacDonald says, "The question is not will God answer our prayers, but do we have faith to petition Him persistently?"[2] Luke put it this way, "when the Son of Man comes, will He find faith on the earth?" (Luke 18:8, NASB) We've heard it said, *"seeing is believing,"* but I suggest the opposite is even more realistic, *"believing is seeing."* Exercising faith means we "see" it with our *"mind's eye"* even before it ever happens. I am convinced that the good people of my congregation would not want a pastor who did not view the church through eyes of such great faith. But what wouldn't I give to have a church full of people who see things the same way?

I believe Elijah *"saw"* fire fall from heaven or he would have never taken on 450+ phony preachers all by himself. I am convinced David *"saw"* Goliath fall to the ground with a thud or he would have never stepped out from an Israeli line armed with only a rock and a sling. The apostle John was exiled to a rock island all alone because of his faith, yet when Sunday came without a preacher or a choir or a congregation, the Scripture says he was "in the Spirit on the Lord's Day." (Revelation 1:10) I believe John *"saw"* something with anointed eyes of faith.

Is that the way you *"see?"* Is the glass half full or half empty? In your view, is everything positive or negative?

Are you optimistic or are you a pessimist? One of my men testified recently on a Wednesday night. He and his wife had gone to Indianapolis for the Bill Gaither Concert. They had inadvertently parked in a tow zone, and sure enough, when they returned late that night, there was no car. I think he told us it cost something like $175 to get their vehicle back but then he added, "At least it saved us the $10 parking fee!"

Sunday School teacher, do you "see" your class continually growing until you will need to search for a bigger classroom? Mom and Dad, do you "see" your children growing up to accept Jesus as Savior and serve Him? Do you "see" that prodigal son or daughter coming back to Christ and living a life that is altogether different? Do you "see" the outcome of your surgery or treatment in a positive way, regardless of what the doctor has said? It is absolutely imperative that we Christians develop spiritual eyes that can see supernaturally and keep us encouraged and believing that God really is able.

Wayne is a member of my church. When his nurse-daughter saw him as he officiated a Saturday morning high school soccer game and noticed how jaundiced he looked, she insisted he go to the emergency room, so he did, I think mostly to keep peace in the family. Prodding. Poking. Probing. Pancreatic cancer. That's usually a death sentence but in this case, Wayne possessed too much faith in a powerful God to give in to such notion.

After surgery, the chemotherapy began. Doctors had told Wayne up front, "We're going to make you really sick." However, they are baffled by the fact that throughout the entire treatment, Wayne was never sick nor did he ever feel badly. It's now over a couple of years later. The chemo is over. Looking a little thinner, Wayne gives God the glory in his Wednesday night testimonies at church. He is a walking miracle and everyone knows it, including Wayne. I am so glad a man of such faith is a member of "the pastor's prayer partners," a group of faithful men who lay hands on me and pray for me every Sunday morning before worship.

Elisha and his servant were surrounded by the enemy, but surrounding the enemy were the forces of God: horses and chariots of fire! Answering the request of the prophet, the Aramean army was struck with blindness and Elisha led them—all the way into the city of Syria, the capital of Israel. God then opened their eyes and they discovered they had been delivered into the hands of their enemy.

What would happen if we all really began to be more optimistic in our faith? I am convinced that one's attitude makes a tremendous difference in that person's future. I've seen people with terminal illnesses basically give up and die because that's what is expected of them. I've seen others refuse to buckle under defeat and rise above it all, probably adding months, if not years, to their lives. What if you decided you are bigger than what has a grip on you because your God is bigger? What if you made up your mind that you are going to lead that lost person to Christ no matter how often they refuse your invitations to church? What if you really believed in your heart that God is truly bigger than what's the matter? What if …?

Too many people justify everything that takes place in their lives with the notion, *everything happens for a reason*. I've heard that idea pronounced in lots of places including private residences, hospital waiting rooms, and, worst of all, funeral homes. This belief, one that greatly upsets me, is such a blatant lie of Satan. We are so prone to have to blame someone, but we cannot blame God for all that happens in life. Life isn't all "programmed" to be. We have the power to change the future through praying to Almighty God, the One Who actually makes changes. But before it will ever happen, we must be able to visualize it in our minds and hold onto that dream with all that's within us.

We've learned a valuable lesson from the servant of a prophet of God: Believing really is seeing. Perhaps you're in a tough spot. Things are going against you. The future is looking bleak. King Nebuchadnezzar was having nightmares and was hoping Daniel could help interpret his wild dreams. The prophet, however, would not take any credit for what he could or couldn't do. Instead, he pointed the king to One Who was greater: "but there is a God in heaven." (Daniel 2:28, NRSV) There's the answer for you and me in our dilemma. Such great faith.

Walt Disney died before Disney World in Orlando was completed. Somewhere I read that on opening day in 1971, five years after Disney's death, someone said to Mike Vance, Creative Director of Disney Studios, "Isn't it too bad Walt Disney didn't live to see this?" Vance's reply: "He did see it—that's why it's here!"

CHAPTER EIGHT

JESUS FROWNS on FAITHLESSNESS

You of little faith, why did you doubt?
(Matthew 14:31, NRSV)

When I was a student in high school, I only wanted one thing—I wanted out! Toward the end of my junior year, a buddy of mine and I discovered that we only needed two classes to graduate, and they were both being offered in summer school,   so we quickly enrolled. In those days, graduating early was brand new territory, at least for East Atlanta High School. They told us it was a possibility, but that if we did graduate early, we would not be allowed to come back a year later and "walk" with our class. We couldn't care less about "walking," so we accepted the stipulation and our commencement consisted of a Coke party in the teachers' lounge on a hot day in August. The principal and guidance counselor gave each of us a king-sized bottle of Coca Cola, right out of the machine, and presented our diplomas as the two of us sat at a lunch table.

So it had been almost six years since that high school graduation party and my pastor was trying to persuade me to go to college! As mentioned earlier, Pastor Bennett Dudney had been doing his best to talk me into enrolling in our denominational school in Nashville. I will admit it as loudly as I can; I was faithless! For several reasons, an under graduate program for me was a ridiculous idea. I covered a few of them on the beginning pages of this book, but there were a couple of other reasons I failed to mention...

Number one, I assumed I was too old. Everyone else in college was fresh out of high school. Having been "on my own" for over five years, I had lived in my own apartment a mile or so away from the house of my childhood. I did what I pleased and whenever I wanted to do it. I went wherever I wanted to go with no one's permission or approval. I had grown accustomed to relying upon no one for anything. When I thought about being a resident student at a college in another state, I wasn't so sure about dormitory life and all the rules and regulations that go along with it.

As a matter of fact, when I did get to college, one of the things I had to agree to was "room check" every night at 11 p.m. Our resident assistant would come and knock on our door to make sure my roommate and I were present and accounted for. On many nights, after the R.A. left, so did I! Being the school photographer, I would often go to the darkroom of the yearbook office located in the basement of old McClurkan Auditorium. Always with a deadline to make, I worked late many nights, developing film and printing pictures, but without a pass. I would hear the security guard come through the building about midnight and I would get really quiet as he checked the doors. Once all was "secure," he placed the padlocks on the doors at both ends of the building so no one could get in—or out!

Around 2 a.m. my work would be finished, and I would be ready to go back to my room in Wise Hall. Leaving the yearbook office, I would carefully go down the darkened hallway to the staircase and feel my way along the wall, up the creepy, creaky old stairs to the balcony of the auditorium. At the end of the balcony, I stood in the shadows and watched out the window until the security guard passed below in his little white golf cart. I then opened the window, exited, climbed down the fire escape as far as I could go, and dropped to the ground. I then ran across campus in the night, back to my dorm.

In that day, a few of the campus cops were retired preachers. One particular night, one of them caught me like a rat in a trap. I had gone through my usual routine and was headed back to my dorm in the wee hours of the morning when he seemed to come out of nowhere on his little white vehicle. He stopped me and asked to see my pass for being out after hours, something I did not possess. Instead, I started to testify to him about some of the miraculous things God had been doing in my life. My guard-friend got so blessed that he forgot why he had stopped me, and after a few minutes of visitation and jubilation, I went my way and he went his, both of us rejoicing in the Lord!

Reason number two for not going to college, I wasn't entirely convinced I could make the grade. Grade wise, I did alright in high school but never made any honor rolls. Then again, I didn't try very hard. The closer I got to realizing that college was, in fact, the will of God for me, the more I wished that I had paid more attention in the classrooms of days gone by. So there I was, a Christian young man who wanted to please God with every waking hour of the day, yet living in a state of faithlessness, something that so displeased my Savior.

As I read my Bible, I noticed a pattern that seemed to emerge from the Gospels. Jesus would teach His disciples a lesson, then send His boys out for a "pop quiz!" Our Lord knew the men He mentored had to learn the lesson of faith and trust right away in their journey, if they were going to make it. Jim Cymbala wrote, "The enemy knows that the best way to breach your spiritual immune system is by attacking your faith. Once your faith is undermined, you become an easy target for a variety of spiritual maladies."[1] Therefore, Jesus helped His followers by providing occasional obstacle courses. One of the best examples of this divine testing process is Matthew, chapter 8. Jesus had just finished his powerful Sermon on the Mount which included incredible insight on prayer, fasting, and not only believing *in* God but simply *believing* God. He then threw in a few extra lessons as His followers observed some real life situations…

Evidently having heard the stories of the miraculous power of Jesus of Nazareth, a leper came to Christ with a strong belief that the Healer could make him well. Brother Matthew tells us that Jesus agreed and did the unthinkable thing—He actually touched this diseased person. Lepers in that day lived in colonies because they were considered to be outcasts. If one came down the road toward you, he or she had to cross the road and even yell out a warning, "Unclean!" Most of them wore a mask to prevent others from breathing the same air they had exhaled. And heaven forbid, under no circumstances would you ever intentionally, on purpose, touch a real live leper! Jesus did. Jesus did the unthinkable thing: He just reached right out and touched a leper! The former tax collector recording the event then says, "Immediately his leprosy was cleansed." (Matthew 8:3)

A soldier in charge of a hundred others approached Jesus. Back at the home place, this decorated hero of the nation had a servant who was extremely ill, even paralyzed. Once made aware of the need, Jesus was ready to follow the officer home, but the centurion stopped him, articulating that the only thing needed was for Jesus to say the word and his servant would be made well. Impressed and pleased with the soldier's faith, Jesus spoke that word and Matthew announces, "his servant was healed that same hour." (Matthew 8:13)

After the phenomenal healing of the soldier's servant, Jesus and a few of His friends went to the home of Simon Peter. There, in a back room of the house, they found Peter's mother-in-law, feverish and extremely ill. The gospel writer doesn't elaborate on the illness, but it sounds pretty serious. According to the Scripture, Jesus went into the lady's room, "touched her hand and the fever left her." (Matthew 8:15) The dear sister even felt so much better that she got up from her sick bed and began to serve her guests.

After a few individual miracles here and there, it was almost as if Jesus had hung a shingle out the window and opened for business. People started showing up at His door for healing of all kinds. He was curing people right and left, even casting evil spirits out of many who had been tormented. No one was turned away. Matthew summed it all up with the words, "He cast out spirits with a word and healed all who were sick." (Matthew 8:16)

In another place he wrote, "great multitudes followed Him, and He healed them all." (Matthew 12:15) Again and again, Jesus publicly demonstrated that He had the power to heal the sick, cast out demons, even raise the dead. Having been privy to all of these experiences, the disciples of Christ had no excuse for not exercising great faith. Nazarene professor and Bible scholar Frank Moore encourages the disciple of today: "Expect to be amazed. There are many things in life I don't know or understand. But one thing I'm sure of: God will amaze you when you embark on a quest of discovery with Him."[2]

Remember when computer games were the new fad? Among others, I recall playing *Frogger* and *Pac Man* and, oh yes, *Donkey Kong*. There was one game where the "enemy" was shooting something at you and you had to fire back, hitting his bullets or missiles or whatever they were in mid-air before they hit you. It was fairly easy at first, just stopping those shots one at a time, but once you graduated to another level, you suddenly found yourself bombarded with enemy fire. As the music's tempo increased, so did the rival assault, not to mention your blood pressure. Those missiles started to come toward you more than one at a time and at increasing speed. As a matter of fact, you had to keep moving to the right and to the left to keep the artillery from hitting their intended target—you!

That's how I view what has just happened with Jesus and His companions in Matthew, chapter eight. The disciples had listened to their Master's powerful preaching with specifics about prayer and believing. They had witnessed miracles involving a leper, a soldier's servant, and an in-law of one of their own. After a few isolated cases, suddenly these guys go to a higher level, witnessing crowds of needy people converging on Christ. He heals people, He performs miracles, He astonishes the multitudes. They approach Him from all directions and He never misses a beat. These disciples had been there. They had witnessed everything. They had taken it all in, every healing, every deliverance, every miracle. There's no other way to say it, they had seen the tremendous power of Almighty God.

It was now time for those disciples to advance, to show-case what they had gleaned from the Master. It's not a ceremony of commencement in a crowded auditorium; it isn't even a pop party in a teacher's lounge. Jesus announces that they are going to the other side of a lake. Matthew uses the word "commanded." (Matthew 8:18) Tired and worn out but without a worry in the world, Jesus goes to sleep at one end of the boat. Suddenly, a storm blows up. Among the disciples: a doctor, a tax collector, and perhaps another person or two of a particular profession, but I think it's safe to say that most of them were sun-bronzed fishermen.

A storm on the sea was nothing novel to these guys. They knew what to do with the sail, which way to turn the rudder, and even how to bail water. But this storm was different. This tempest was like no other. Water started to overtake the boat, faster than they could dish it out. The tiny vessel was being tossed by the angry waves, up and down, back and forth, right and left, much worse than *The Minnow* on *Gilligan's Island*. They could hardly hear the alarmed voices of one another amidst the loud, howling winds, the crashing waves, and the frightening creaks of the boards that held their craft together. Terrified for their lives, those water-soaked sailors with their wet garments stuck to their skin frantically awakened Jesus from His slumber.

Surrounded by his drenched disciples, Jesus arose and faced those dark, billowing, angry clouds. With His wet hair blowing in the wind and speeding water droplets stinging His face, our Lord commanded and demanded the storm to cease. Probably much quicker than it had blown in, the wind subsided, the waves died down, and I believe, the sun peeked out to shine. Jesus had proven to His friends that He truly was the Master, Master of the sea, Master of the weather, Master of everything! But just before He calmed that storm, He had spoken some cutting words to His faithful band of students: "Why are you fearful, O you of little faith?" (Matthew 8:26) Eugene Peterson has Jesus calling them "cowards" and "faint-hearts." (The Message) That was our Savior's way of saying, "Boys, you flunked the test!"

One can almost hear the disappointment in the Voice of our Lord as He sincerely addresses His men. They had been eye witnesses to some incredible events and now they're given a test and they don't do so well. It was as if they had forgotten the sights, the sounds, and the smells; they had blocked everything they had experienced.

I'll talk more about "the test of faith" in chapter thirteen but let me ask you, have you ever failed an exam, and if so, how did you feel? I mentioned that I had gone to college six years after high school, a move I felt almost to be too late. Well, I can now top that. I went to seminary twenty-five years later! I had completed a 30-hour Master of Church Management but then, in my fifties, I enrolled at Nazarene Theological Seminary for a Master of Divinity, a 90-hour program. What was I thinking?

The program required a two-week visit to NTS twice a year. Following the syllabus for one particular class, I had purchased the needed books and did much of the reading before I left Oklahoma for Kansas City. Among the reading lists were two books on church history, both 400-some pages thick. As I went from station to station in the registration line on day one of seminary, a lady across the table inquired about my classes. I told her I was taking *Heritage I* with Dr. Paul Bassett. She burst into laughter as I went to the next station. There I was asked the same question which drew the same response! A third person followed suit. It was becoming more plain to me that Dr. Bassett, a highly intelligent professor of church history, had the reputation of being a tough teacher. I suggested to one of the registrars that perhaps I needed to drop that class. She asked if I had read both those books to which I explained that I was only halfway through the first. She then warned me that I was in trouble!

Seeing a professor with whom I once pastored, I told him the reaction I had been getting. He asked about my class and instructor and when I told him, he laughed as well! As I mentioned I was considering dropping the class, he advised me to stick with it but with the attitude, *I'm gonna learn something from this guy.*

The next morning I attended my first class in *Heritage I*, finding that Dr. Bassett was an extraordinary lecturer. He made the stories of our early religious fathers come alive in our classroom. He explained that there was one big test over the 800 pages of the two textbooks and that we would individually schedule when we wanted to take it. On our first attempt (and he made it sound like none of us would pass), we had to get 70% correct. On our second try, it was 80% and finally on the last time we would have to answer 90% right in order to pass. I knew I was sunk!

Discovering a drugstore a few blocks away at the bottom of the hill, I walked down there one afternoon and purchased a package of index cards. I filled them up with dates and other pertinent data on historical events from the books. Finding an unused classroom in the basement of the seminary building, I lined a huge conference table with my cards in chronological order. I did my best to memorize all those dates, places, persons, and whatever else I needed to know. Once I felt I was "ready," I went to the prof's office to request an exam and completed it to the best of my ability.

The next afternoon I was studying in the library when Dr. Bassett came in, straight to me. "You had a tough time with that test, didn't you?" Not yet sure of my score, I agreed. He replied, "Well, you can have a second chance whenever you are ready." Suddenly, I was aware of the vicinity of my grade!

I read, I studied, I memorized, I recited, and oh yes, I prayed! I made my way up the stairs to the third floor once again and took the test. Although I still have no idea what the score was, this time I passed! I felt like God had helped me, but I know He only helps those who help themselves.

Faith is a huge part of the journey. God wants us to exercise faith in Him and believe Him to perform great miracles in our lives. Dr. Neil B. Wiseman wrote:

> The record is amazing—what seemed impossible has been accomplished. Little has become much. Small has grown to big. Tough has become tender. Across two millennia, God's power working through human beings has transformed apparent impossibilities into glorious victories.[3]

Aren't you grateful we serve a big God?

CHAPTER NINE

HOW MUCH is ENOUGH?

If you have faith as small as a mustard seed ...

(Luke 17:6, NIV)

If my memory serves me correctly, it was a package of petunia seeds. I picked them out at the store myself, mainly because the colorful picture on the front of the envelope had caught my eye. It was a grade school home-work assignment, fourth grade, I believe. We were to plant some flower seeds in our yards and report their progress to the class week-by-week. Remembering how the teacher had stressed that we were to do this all by ourselves with no parental help, I headed out to the spot in our backyard that my Dad had shown me, flower seeds in one hand, a small pick in the other. I began to dig. And I dug.

I dug and I dug. That hole must have been at least a foot-and-a-half deep, if not two. It goes without mentioning that this was my first attempt at planting flowers. I carefully poured the seeds into the hole and buried them with dirt. Daily, I faithfully watered my seeds and watched them, but never did I see any flowers. It's now a half century later and I wouldn't be surprised if those pretty petunias are still struggling with all their might to push up through that Georgia red clay!

Well, that disastrous attempt to grow flowers was unsuccessful because I had buried those seeds way too deep in the ground. I don't remember the grade I received on the assignment but it was probably right in line with the rest of my science grades. There was another time, however, when I made another effort using my limited agricultural talent, a disaster that was altogether different. This time I was grown and married, living in a Nazarene parsonage in Columbus, Nebraska. It's the Midwest, farmland of America. The dirt is so black there, it looks like potting soil. Surely, anyone could grow a crop there. Missing my southern okra long enough, I had decided to grow some.

Knowing that Charlie in my church had a tiller, I asked him to bring it by and turn over a small piece of our backyard for me, about ten feet square. I just wanted a little patch to set out some tomato plants and a few rows of okra. After my friend had completed his part, it was now my turn. I had purchased a package of okra seeds and, following the directions on the package, I began strategically placing them about every two inches along a little row I had dug. I kept thinking about how tiny those seeds were, however, and I couldn't imagine one of them was powerful enough to produce any kind of crop. Therefore, thinking there is strength in numbers, I began to intentionally spill those tiny okra seeds up and down the trenches I had dug. I buried them, watered them, and watched for them to grow. It wasn't long before my okra plants made their debut under the Nebraska sun, but instead of coming up as individual plants, they grew in bushes, all intertwined together. It didn't take them long to choke each other out, and I was left still without my southern delight.

Over the years, I've used those two illustrations in sermons I've preached and the biggest laughs have always come from the farmers in my congregations. My mistake with the petunias was a hole too deep, and my error with the okra was too many seeds planted too close together. I guess one must have the accurate depth, the proper amount, the right combination for nature to work. What about faith? Can we have too much? Is there such a thing as too little?

As we read the words of Jesus and follow His teachings, we quickly discover that one does not need an abundance of faith in order for God to move. In Luke's gospel, Jesus says, "If you have faith as small as a mustard seed, you can say to this mulberry tree, 'Be uprooted and planted in the sea,' and it will obey you." (Luke 17:6, NIV) Eugene Peterson translates that verse a little differently: "But the Master said, 'You don't need more faith. There is no "more" or "less" in faith. If you have a bare kernel of faith, say the size of a poppy seed, you could say to this sycamore tree, 'Go jump in the lake,' and it would do it.'" (Luke 17:6. MSG)

We were visiting our son and daughter-in-law in southern California and were riding with Tommy in his shiny black Ford F-150 pickup truck. Sandie was in the passenger seat and I was in the back, where I was becoming more and more claustrophobic with each mile. Our son had been hired to play percussion for a musical production at California Baptist University in Riverside, and we were on our way to one of the performances. About twenty minutes out of Tustin, Tommy's truck began to slow down as if it was going to stop. He took the next exit just to get off the interstate, and we chugged along for several yards until we found a small parking lot at a medical facility, a safe place to pull over. With the help of the internet on his cell phone, our son found a nearby 76 Station with mechanics on duty.

After talking briefly with one of the repairmen on the phone, Tommy drove toward that location in our struggling vehicle. With the truck parked in the drive outside the bay, the mechanic lifted the hood and attached his computer in order to diagnose our dilemma. Sandie was already praying, "Lord, make it inexpensive and make it small!"

Based on our description of the problem, the repairman's first thought was the alternator, and I knew from firsthand experience that if that was indeed the problem, we would be talking big money. As we waited for the expert to read the data on his hand-held device, I'm thinking, *We could put this on our credit card...* Sandie was still praying, "Lord, make it inexpensive and make it small!" The mechanic walked away and disappeared into the garage. He returned moments later, did something to the vehicle, then turned to us and in broken English said, "Blowed fuse in computer, you free to go!" He left. We stood there, looking at one another. My son and I walked back into the garage to find out what we owed them, but they insisted there was no charge!

Almost in shock, we climbed into the truck and headed for the freeway. I mentioned that we could have laid down some big bucks back there for a huge mechanical problem but instead it was a quick fix and even one that was on the house. It was then that Sandie informed us of her prayer of great faith, "Lord, make it inexpensive and make it small!" That's when Tommy and I broke out together in singing "The Doxology". We stopped halfway through and invited his Mom to join us but all she could do was cry! What we thought could have been a major repair job only took a tiny and evidently, free fuse to fix.

Every year in September we have a very special Sunday at our church. It's the day of our annual healing service, one that we take very seriously. As a matter of fact, we begin to pray about this particular day weeks in advance. Everyone is thinking about it. The entire congregation is praying about it. People are united together in one spirit, anticipating mighty miracles at the hand of Almighty God. All are excited about what God is going to do in our church on that special day.

Our congregational singing for that morning is geared toward God's miraculous power. I always preach a biblical message on healing, usually from stories like Jesus' healing of blind Bartimaeus or the woman who touched the hem of His garment or the times when our Lord touched the multitudes and made a significant difference in their lives. After I preach, there is always an altar call but this one is different from other public invitations. Every ordained elder or licensed minister in our congregation comes to the front of the sanctuary armed with small vials of oil. The invitation is given for people to come forward to be anointed for healing— physical healing, yes, but also for other kinds of healing. They come for emotional, marital, and spiritual healing. They come for the healing of their homes or their finances. Whatever is the matter in a person's life, that's the reason for their response. Each seeker selects one of the ministers who then anoints that person with oil and prays the prayer of faith. Why do we do that? It's because the Bible instructs us to do so. "Are you sick? Call the church leaders together to pray and anoint you with oil in the name of the Master." (James 5:14, MSG)

Oil has always represented the Holy Spirit in the Scriptures. Remember the parable of the bridesmaids in Matthew, chapter 25? Five were wise and had their lamps burning brightly, ready to go and meet the bridegroom whenever he called. The others were considered foolish because they had forgotten to get oil for their lamps. When the call finally came, the foolish virgins wanted to borrow or buy oil but it was too late. Jamieson, Fausset, and Brown comment on the *oil* of this story:

> *This supply of oil, then, representing that inward grace which distinguishes the wise, must denote, more particularly, that 'supply of the Spirit of Jesus Christ,' which, as it is the source of the new spiritual life at the first, is the secret of its enduring character. Everything short of this*

may be possessed by 'the foolish'; while it is the possession of this that makes 'the wise' to be 'ready' when the Bridegroom appears, and fit to 'go in with Him to the marriage.'[1]

Therefore, when we bring anointing oil into the picture, we are introducing the very Spirit of the Living God, the One Who has power to perform miracles.

But is it necessary that we have the "right" kind of oil? Does it need to be oil from the Middle East that can be purchased in many Christian bookstores? Or is it okay to use everyday olive oil that we find on the shelf of the Walmart? Personally, I am a stronger proponent for the emphasis being put on the anointing in faith rather than the brand or kind of oil applied. As a matter of fact, that verse in James 5 about the leaders of the church anointing the sick with oil is followed a couple of verses later with, "The prayer of the righteous is powerful and effective." (James 5:16, NRSV)

Several years ago, Sandie and I were in our second pastorate, a congregation of forty people in Columbus, Nebraska. God had been really blessing our services. People were responding to invitations to the altar almost every week. We saw some saved, some were sanctified wholly, others had needs of all kinds met at the hand of our powerful God. But in the midst of a perpetual revival, something suddenly happened to my wife and me. It was as if God had withdrawn Himself from both of us, and at the same time. We prayed, she taught, I preached, and it was like a blanket was lifted, but only for those moments, then replaced. We went through the entire week without either of us personally sensing His

Presence. This went on for weeks, for months. As a matter of fact, our own sense of godlessness lasted for six months of what we called *"the dark night of the soul."* And oddly enough, we both experienced it together.

We had done nothing wrong. On the contrary, we were doing everything right. My wife kept teaching Sunday School; and I continued to preach the Word. I was calling on our people. We were praying and having daily devotions. We kept doing what we knew God would want, except we didn't *feel* Him. We were clearly unable to acknowledge His presence. The reason we continued on and didn't give up is because we had both learned a long time ago that the Christian life is lived by faith, not by feeling. But it sure is more encouraging when a Christian senses His Spirit.

The annual district Pastors and Spouses' Retreat came along in the fall. We had to be there. We were so dry spiritually—we needed to experience God again. We rode with another pastor and his wife from Nebraska to Colorado Springs for the retreat which was being held at Glen Eyrie, home of the Navigators. Our speaker was the Nazarene General Superintendent who had ordained me, Dr. Eugene L. Stowe. We so anticipated his messages for those three days.

Upon our arrival, however, Sandie became tremendously dizzy. She was lying down in our room which, for her, continued to spin around. Time was drawing close for the opening session of our retreat. My wife mentioned that she did not want to miss that service, how she needed to be there and was determined to attend, even if I had to hold her up. I knew we needed to pray but I also realized this called for desperate measures, it called for an anointing. Since

I don't usually travel with anointing oil, I asked Sandie if she had any kind of oil in her purse. She searched through her bag and the only thing she could find was a small bottle of hand lotion. I said, "That will work!" Together we prayed the prayer of faith, believing God was touching her and relieving her of the vertigo, as I anointed her in the Name of Jesus— with hand lotion!

We made it downstairs to the place of worship and even arrived a few minutes early. Since the room seemed to be a bit stuffy, we wandered out on the veranda to get some air. One could not help but notice the beautiful star-speckled Colorado sky. As we looked up and stared at God's wonderful creation, all of a sudden, He was there! For the first time in six months, we both sensed the presence of the Spirit of God once again! We started to laugh, we cried, we made so much noise that a couple of people came out to see what was going on. "We're just having revival!," we said. The *"dark night of the soul"* had ended!

Sandie and I were recently on a Disney World vacation— just the two of us! It was the year of our daughter-in-law's family Christmas, our very first one without our son, and we needed a big distraction, so we flew to Orlando for a week. I was awakened at 2 a.m. by a phone call from a lady in our church back home in Indiana. Someone was in the E.R. with a stroke. Feeling very badly that I could not rush to the hospital as I normally would do, I explained that I was out of town but would certainly pray.

Once the sun was up and we were about to begin our day, I sent a text message to Andrew Hall, our Youth Pastor, and asked him to go to the hospital. Andrew and his fiancé were in his truck headed to Muncie but they turned around and aimed for Indy's St. Vincent Hospital. After I contacted the family to tell them I was sending Pastor Andrew in my place, they called Andrew on his cell phone, requesting he bring some oil to anoint their loved one. Since they were nowhere near home, Andrew and Sidney had no opportunity to retrieve any anointing oil from the church.

Once they exited the interstate, they spotted a pharmacy near the hospital. Pastor Andrew ran inside looking for olive oil only to find none. What he did discover, however, was a small bottle of canola oil and a container of Johnson's baby shampoo. He made his purchase and within minutes, they arrived at the medical center and Andrew darted into the men's room. He quickly emptied the contents of the shampoo bottle and replaced it with canola oil, then the twosome headed for the elevator. Andrew texted me later: *I didn't have any anointing oil so I had to improvise with a bottle of canola oil and a travel-sized shampoo bottle from Walgreens.* Well, God answered prayer and within a couple of weeks the patient was moved to a skilled facility in our town for a month or so with full recovery expected.

In both of these situations, I don't think God cared if we had used common olive oil from our kitchen cabinet, special oil imported from Israel, or cucumber melon-scented hand lotion from a lady's Vera Bradley handbag. I think the only thing that concerned the Lord was that we had heeded His admonition from the Scriptures to anoint the sick in the Name of Jesus and that we exercised great faith in the healing powers of the Great Physician. He answers our prayers of faith.

For what do you need to pray today? Is there a physical illness or a marriage that's on the rocks or the need for a job? Is it a financial matter or one of an emotional nature or do you just need divine direction in your life? Perhaps you need to share your concern with others or maybe you need an anointing from a leader of the church. The one thing we do know is that faith is both needed and required. How much is needed? Only the amount that you have within.

The key concept to keep in mind is that we must maintain a close personal relationship with the Father. Going through some things in a drawer, I found a handwritten note from our son, Tommy, written in 1994 at age seven. He had flown with his Mom to Oklahoma because Sandie's mother was having surgery. He printed the following words on a small piece of paper and apparently Sandie mailed it to me:

Thursday night, July 7, '94, from Tommy

> *I am having a good time in Oklahoma City. And on Monday night my stomach hurt and I got sick. And the next night I got sick. And every night I got sick. And I didn't get sick on Wednesday night. And I'm missing you very very much daddy. Love, Tommy*

Well, I don't even need to mention the fact that I was also missing him. When we are estranged from the Father, hopefully, we are missing Him but we can be sure that He is missing us. He wants to provide for us, to answer our prayers, to do great and mighty things in our lives on a regular basis. But we must be close enough to hear Him and to exercise faith—not volumes of it, just whatever amount we might have. All it takes, according to Jesus, is "faith as small as a mustard seed." (Luke 17:6, NIV) In other words, exercise the faith that is already within. The response is powerful!

CHAPTER TEN

BUT WHAT IF...

For still the vision awaits its appointed time;
it hastens to the end—it will not lie.
If it seems slow, wait for it;
it will surely come; it will not delay.
(Habakkuk 2:3, ESV)

The Cleveland Clinic. I have heard about it but never had experienced it until today. Actually, I drove over to Cleveland, Ohio from New Castle, Indiana yesterday and spent the night in a hotel. I made a test run last night to The Surgery Center so I would know where to go this morning. Someone told me this entire facility spreads out over 140 acres and I believe it, for I've already been lost a few times this afternoon.

So here I sit in the Surgical Family Lounge of The Cleveland Clinic, writing chapter ten of my book. A man from my church is having brain surgery. I met Bob and his family here this morning at 9:30 a.m. He was taken back for preparation at 10:30 and around 11 a.m. I had the privilege of reading Scripture to him and praying the prayer of faith. Then we waited for them to take him to surgery. And we waited. Noon came and went. Then it was 1 p.m. Next came 2 p.m. With nothing by mouth since midnight, Bob was becoming hungrier and growing more thirsty by the minute. Members of the family, including myself, took turns running to lunch and back. We were told that "a surgeon" was having problems in the operating room, the one that was needed for my friend's procedure. It occurred to me that we should be praying for that other surgeon.

Finally, at about 2:30 p.m. they came for Bob. We had waited some five hours from the time of our arrival. Now we wait for the three-to-four hour surgery to be completed. And a little later, we discover the surgery didn't actually begin until 4:34, two hours after he was taken back. It's hard to wait. Even Bob was admittedly nervous and becoming more and more anxious as the day wore on.

My father-in-law was a great man and he and I had lots of memorable times together. We used to go shopping, the four of us—Sandie, her parents, and me. While Sandie and her Mom were in the stores, Tom and I would sit on a mall bench and he'd say to me, "Alright, I'm going to teach you how to wait." We would sit there for what seemed like hours, perhaps days. We would watch people coming from one direction, make a few "wise" comments about them, then look the other way and do the same with those shoppers approaching from the opposite direction. Tom is now wait-ing for us in heaven. In the mean time, I've had opportunity to hand down his waiting instructions to my own son—passing on the baton. It's still hard to wait.

That's pretty much what a pastor does—wait. Oh, I get to study and preach. I pray and dream and try to find God's will for the future of the church. I visit in homes and hospitals and try to help people to grow spiritually. But much of my job is waiting—waiting in hospital waiting rooms, waiting in funeral homes, waiting in airports, waiting on God. I joke with people that the only exercise I get is jumping to conclusions. One of my associate pastors recently went to a hospital to sit with a family for an early morning surgery. The time of surgery kept getting bumped back due to emergencies and whatever. They finally did the operation after 5 p.m. The problem with waiting is that it gives a person more time to think about the situation and to doubt.

I think one reason it is so difficult to sit during a surgery is because we are already concerned about the outcome. With all the faith in the world, we are still human and if we are not careful, we will allow our minds to play-out all the possible scenarios, including the ones that are not encouraging. What if the doctor finds this? What if it turns into that? What if there's trouble with anesthesia? What if they don't get it all? What if? … Would you say that is a lack of trust? As we pray and linger for God's answer, we are tempted to doubt. Again, is that a lack of faith in the Lord's power?

Habakkuk was a prophet of God in seventh century B.C. during the reign of King Manasseh. Looking out across the wicked world of that day, the preacher saw violence, injustice, spoiling, strife, contention—if it was sinful, Habakkuk witnessed it. The law had not been enforced, therefore, iniquity abounded. There was no legal protection for the innocent folk who were sentenced as "guilty" in courts that were manipulated by selfish lawyers and cruel officials. Aren't you thankful we who live in America have never seen anything like that? The entire nation was suffering because of the evils of government, yet God seemed to be doing nothing about it.

Now we must understand that most prophets in that day were bold and in your face, but not Brother Habakkuk. His style was to speak to God much more than he spoke to people! He even taught that it's okay to occasionally question our Creator! If anyone has any doubts or concerns about anything, Habakkuk helps us here, for God had a special plan for His chosen one.

Once in trouble, the prophet pushes the panic button! "O Lord, how long shall I cry for help, and you will not listen? Or cry to you 'Violence!' and you will not save?" (Habakkuk 1:2, NRSV) I like the way Eugene Peterson translates: "How many times do I have to yell, 'Help! Murder! Police!' before you come to the rescue?" (Habakkuk 1:2, MSG) God's surprising solution for a troubled Judah was to send a bigger and more frightening nation to do the correcting. I think we can understand why Habakkuk is puzzled: "Lord, do You know what You're doing? What if they never listen?"

One Commentator wrote: "A burning question remained in Habakkuk's heart. Why would the everlastingly preeminent Yahweh, the absolutely Holy One, the immutably permanent Rock, utilize so wicked a people to administer discipline on Judah?"[1] Why would God use a godless nation to punish a godly nation? God always has a plan, but that divine plan doesn't always make sense! God's plan for Joshua was to destroy Jericho by marching around the city and blowing trumpets! God's plan for Gideon was to defeat the 135,000-strong marauding Midianites with only three hundred soldiers! God's plan for the disciples of Jesus was to feed 5,000 men plus their wives and children with a little lad's lunch. As ridiculous as it might sometimes sound, God always has a plan. "'For I know the plans I have for you,' declares the Lord, 'plans to prosper you and not to harm you, plans to give you hope and a future.'" (Jeremiah 29:11, NKJV) The prophet didn't understand and you and I may not either!

God seems to be into the waiting game! "Wait for the Lord; be strong and take heart and wait for the Lord." (Psalm 27:4, NIV) "Be still before the Lord and wait patiently for him; do not fret when men succeed in their ways, when they carry out their wicked schemes." (Psalm 37:7, NIV) There are so many times when it seems God doesn't even hear us! "O Lord, how long shall I cry, And You will not hear?" (Habakkuk 1:2a) We know the Bible teaches us to watch and pray, but it's so hard to wait! Jesus told three of his men to "watch and pray, lest you enter into temptation." (Matthew 26:41) They, too, found it difficult to linger and kept falling asleep. We are so tempted to take matters into our own hands! It's just plain hard to wait!

We were once traveling in our car all night to get to Oklahoma from Indiana. Our son, Tommy, was only three years old and we were making our trip at night in hopes that he would sleep all the way. However, somewhere in Missouri he suddenly woke up and wanted out of his confining car seat. His Mom asked, "Do you want to get out for a minute and stretch your legs?" He whimpered, "No, stretch'em out in a bed!" Once I heard his request, I took the very next exit and wheeled into the Do Drop Inn for the night.

It's hard to wait on a position! Two weeks before graduating from college, I sat by the phone every night in my dorm room, waiting for a district superintendent to call! I would soon graduate from college with no place to go. My other friends were getting calls to this church or that ministry—everyone but me. Finally, at almost the last minute he called—no, they called! We received offers of churches from superintendents in North Carolina, Mississippi, and North Florida, all within days of commencement.

It's hard to wait on people! Whenever I need a staff member, I always take my time and pray over the resumes, which I usually take to a church campground or other secluded place where I can spend hours praying in solitude. I may interview three or more candidates, often times several weeks apart. Members of the congregation become nervous, recommending their neighbor's cousin's girl's boyfriend who once gave a devotional at VBS. New staff members have later told me that before I called to offer them a job, they had given up and assumed I had found someone else to fill the position. They had found it difficult to wait on me as I waited on God.

It's hard to wait on a plan! Habakkuk, however, finally discovered that God's plan is always worth the wait! A few years ago, there was an interdenominational program for teenagers called *True Love Waits.* It was designed to encourage teens to practice sexual abstinence in their dating relationships. The program, *True Love Waits,* event-ually became known as *Worth the Wait.* God always has a posi-tion, persons, and a plan just for each of us! We sometimes go through pain, disappointment, and discouragement along the way, making it difficult to wait for God's best. The Bible encourages us: "This vision-message is a witness pointing to what's coming. It aches for the coming—it can hardly wait! And it doesn't lie. If it seems slow in coming, wait. It's on its way. It will come right on time." (Habakkuk 2:3, MSG)

Waiting is a vital part of great faith because it involves trust. According to Nazarene General Superintendent Emeritus, Dr. Stan Toler, "Being a person of faith means being willing to trust God regardless of the outcome."[2] Perhaps that's easier said than done. It may or may not go our way. It may not be for what we had hoped. We probably won't always get what we want but trusting God is always and forever the right thing to do.

Just prior to leaving Oklahoma over six years ago, I join-ed six other men from the church I had pastored for eleven years and we started out at 6 a.m. driving some two hours south to a small Oklahoma town. We were there for the annual Rattlesnake Roundup and boy, were we "pumped!" Although I do have a healthy fear for these reptiles, I've always had a fascination of snakes and for years I've wanted to attend one of these snake hunts. For three weeks I had been watching late-night TV snake-handling shows and I was ready! I saw how Steve Irwin reached into a dark hole in the side of a hill and dragged those rattlers out by the tail, one at a time, rattling all the way!

We arrived on the scene before the booths and vendors were ready, so we wandered around the town until we found a place open that sells fried pies. We each bought one and ate them as we walked along the booths admiring the rattler key rings and necklaces that made an eerie "rattling" sound in the steady Oklahoma wind. Once registered, we were told to drive to the edge of town and get in line, and so we did, becoming part of a ten or twelve car caravan with an ambulance bringing up the rear. We even had a group picture made with the paramedics in front of their emergency vehicle as we waited.

Following a few cars behind the volunteer fireman's pickup truck, we drove five miles out of town and turned onto a lonely country road. About a quarter of a mile down the road we pulled over to the side, stopped, got out of our vehicles, and stood in the middle of the road for instructions. The rough-looking fireman who was in charge had obviously weathered a few snake hunts himself. He had a long gray beard that perfectly matched his long gray hair that was tied behind his head in a thick ponytail. He wore a denim vest that was covered front and back with patches of all sizes, emblems sewn on as badges of courage, each representing snake hunts from all over the country. Everyone listened carefully as the firefighter told us that the recent three-inch rain had driven the snakes into the ground. He said, "They're out there, but you'll have to dig for 'em!" He told us we were allowed to go three miles in a certain direction and warned that we should watch our every step. Then, with no apparent questions, as if firing a gun, he hollered, "Get after it!"

Everyone flew into action, some actually going over the barbed wire, others, like myself, crawling under. We scattered out across the rocky terrain, country that looked like it was out of a TV western—men, women, and children. Believe it or not, I even saw a baby or two in mothers' arms. They carried sticks, buckets, and burlap bags. I started out so carefully strategically placing each step I took: my eyes scanning the ground in all directions, my ears attuned to any sound of warning, adrenaline pumping, my heart pounding. We went down ravines and across creeks and underneath scrub trees. We turned over rocks and used long sticks to dig around in holes. We soon crossed another barbed wire fence, indicating we had passed the first mile mark. Trying to cover a large area, we had scattered, and after keeping my eyes to the ground for awhile, I soon looked up and realized my friends were out of sight and I wasn't even sure of their direction. I was alone—just me and the poisonous serpents!

I made it over the ridge and no one was around. It was hard to believe that two hours had passed. I'd seen three small harmless snakes, a few beetles and scorpions, a skunk, and two rabbits that shot out of the brush right at my feet, momentarily stopping my heart, but no rattlers! I saw everything <u>but</u> a rattlesnake. I had started out being so careful as to where I stepped, but after an hour of nothing, I found myself just carelessly tromping through the brush and the brambles. I turned around and made my way back to the car to wait for my friends.

The rough volunteer fire chief drove up in his pickup truck. He got out, and inquired as to how my hunt had been. As we talked, I heard a rattling noise coming from his truck bed. I walked around the back of his truck and saw two cages with a huge, thick rattlesnake housed in each one. They were monstrous and they were angry. Quick as lightning, one struck at me, leaving a stream of venom running down the chicken wire that kept it encaged. I asked if those snakes were captured in that area on that day but he kept changing the subject and wouldn't answer.

About that time, my friends showed up. They too, were all empty-handed. I shared with them my profound thought—there was not a rattlesnake between there and Texas! The only thing we had to show for our efforts was the stickers in our jeans!

We dragged ourselves back into town, a discouraged lot. There we found an entire carnival going on with hundreds of people crowding the streets and spending their money. A long line of customers awaited their purchase of rattlesnake meat for lunch. For three dollars you could go inside a building and watch a man lie in a canvas bag while seventy-five venomous serpents were placed, one-by-one, inside the bag with him. Everywhere we turned, vendors were making money. We soon became bored and left, heading up the highway for Yukon, agreeing that the best part of the whole trip was the fried pie! Later it dawned on me: The way I felt about that hunt was the way I feel so many times about my church.

Our church is here to reach people for Jesus. Most of our new converts don't just wander into our services, we have to go after them. And when we do go looking for them, not many are just lying around to be caught—we have to dig for them! What if they are not interested? What if they know nothing about church? What if they are offended by my approach? What if they don't respond?

In his book, *Unseen,* Dr. Jack Graham, pastor of one of the nation's largest and most dynamic congregations, Prestonwood Baptist Church just outside Dallas, Texas, writes, "Even the most devoted Christ-followers can't help but wonder sometimes if God really has their backs. Great faith still asks tough questions; great faith still sometimes doubts. Or *often* doubts …"[3]

It takes great faith to see a sinner converted and to be used of the Lord. It takes great faith to see a miracle happen at the Hand of Almighty God. It takes great faith to see our prayers answered and our lives forever changed. It takes great faith to see doubts turn into determination, apprehension turn into belief. It takes great faith to turn our backs on the world and live a Christian life, counting on God to come through for us. It takes great faith to not dwell on the "what ifs?" and concentrate on the promises and power of the One Who died for us. Why don't you give to Jesus all your "what ifs?" at this very moment and begin to trust Him with every part of your life? Your journey with Jesus will take on a new excitement that you've never experienced before.

CHAPTER ELEVEN

SUCH GREAT FAITH

*When Jesus heard it, He marveled, and said
to those who followed, 'Assuredly, I say to you
I have not found such great faith,
not even in Israel!'*
(Matthew 8:10, NKJV)

A Roman legion was comprised of six thousand men who were divided into sixty centuries of one hundred men in each. We use the term *century* for *hundred*. These *centuries* were led by a soldier known as a *centurion*. He was the backbone of the entire army, a man of discipline, the cement that held the whole group together. The centurion was authorized to command, he was always steady in action, and he was ready and willing to die at his post, if need be.

It's very interesting that every centurion appearing in the Bible is mentioned with honor. It was a centurion who suddenly recognized Jesus on the Cross as, in fact, the Son of God. It was Centurion Cornelius who became the first Gentile convert. It was a centurion who discovered the Apostle Paul to be a Roman citizen and rescued him from an angry mob. It was a centurion who had heard that the Jews were out to murder Paul and was able to foil their plans. It was a Roman centurion who was ordered by Felix to look after Paul, and guess who was privileged to go with the apostle on his last missionary journey, treating him with the utmost respect—that's right, a centurion.

In Matthew, chapter 8, a Roman centurion comes to Jesus for help. The thing that was so special about this particular soldier was his attitude toward his servant. (Matthew 8:5-6) Luke tells us that his slave was "ill and close to death." (Luke 7:2) It helps to understand the situation of that day. A slave had no rights whatsoever! Slave owners cared not if a servant lived or died! For this reason, the Apostle Paul advised masters to treat their servants justly and fairly. (Colossians 4:1) And yet, here we see a Roman officer, a leader of the ranks, who is noticeably concerned about the well-being of one who should have never mattered. A few things are worth highlighting about this particular leader.

First, we see that it was not Jesus who approached the soldier but it was the soldier who came to Jesus. Matthew says the officer "came to Him, pleading with Him." (Matthew 8:5) This scene is highly unusual. A man of war going to the Prince of Peace? A Gentile approaching a Jew? That just didn't happen. One must ask why?

It is also interesting that instead of coming in person, Luke's gospel has the centurion sending "Jewish elders" to call on Jesus. (Luke 7:3) Whether our soldier personally paid a visit or sent someone with a message doesn't really matter. The important thing here is that a decorated officer of the feared Roman army was soliciting help from Jesus of Nazareth, the One with a reputation of being a Miracle-worker!

Reading Matthew's narrative, it appears that only one healing had taken place before this particular rendezvous. Matthew records the Sermon on the Mount, followed by the healing of the leper, and then we see the approach of the centurion. In checking a chronological Bible, however, it is clear that the story of the centurion comes only after many different healings! There was the man by the pool at Bethesda, followed by a needy crowd where multiple healings took place, then there's the Sermon on the Mount, bringing us to the incident with the Roman warrior. So Dr. St. Luke's statement about the soldier makes perfect sense: "When he heard about Jesus ..." (Luke 7:3)

Just after my short-lived pro wrestling referee career, I went to see an otolaryngologist (Ear, nose, throat doctor) because I was having continuous breathing problems. It was discovered that without my knowledge, my nose had been broken several times. I knew there had been nights in the ring when I had accidentally gotten in the way of a couple of six-foot bruisers and took a few unexpected blows, but never did I ever imagine my nose had been actually injured.

During the summer after my freshmen year in a Nashville college, I underwent surgery in Atlanta. In my follow-up visit, the doctor assured me that another operation was needed but I had decided after that painful and frustrating ordeal that I was out of the surgery business! Ten years later, still struggling to breathe through my nose, I observed a surgeon at New Hanover Regional Medical Center in Wilmington, North Carolina. On numerous occasions, as I sat with families from my congregation during their medical procedures, I would see this one physician come into the waiting area to give the report to a concerned loved one. I liked his approach to people, how he included children in the consultation, even playing with them on the floor, and someone mentioned that he was an ENT. I made an appointment with him the very next week and he concurred with the doc of a decade back. I was soon scheduled for another rhinoplasty.

The day before the operation, I sat in the office of my new doctor for last minute details. Since many of his patients were children in the market for ear tubes or tonsillectomies, the walls of his exam rooms were decorated with framed pictures—colorful portraits of Goofy, Donald Duck and my favorite Mouse! I very kindly asked him if he had credentials anywhere and he led me to his office where his credentials were on display. Even then, well aware of the answer, I asked him a simple question about my upcoming procedure, "Have you ever done this before?" I needed to hear it straight from the doctor in order to know that I could put my full confidence in this highly recommended surgeon. The Roman c enturion had heard about Jesus of Nazareth and the miracles He had performed, and that was all that was needed for his complete confidence in the Son of God!

That's what faith is all about. The writer to the Hebrews defines faith as "the substance of things hoped for, the evidence of things not seen." (Hebrews 11:1) Vital to the life of a Christian, the words, *faith* and *believe,* are found almost five hundred times in the New Testament.

A walk-through of Hebrews chapter 11 reveals a list of God-fearing individuals with the phrase *by faith* or *through faith* in front of their names. Verse 6 even says one cannot even be converted without exercising faith. The Message translates, "It's impossible to please God apart from faith. And why? Because anyone who wants to approach God must believe both that he exists and that he cares enough to respond." (Hebrews 11:6, MSG)

A careful reading of Matthew's Gospel leaves the reader with the unmistakable idea that the Roman soldier in charge believed in Jesus. Somewhere along the way, he had made a conscious decision to believe in the Son of God. I recently preached the funeral for an 89-year old lady who had been pastorless. Since I did not have the privilege of knowing the deceased, I called the phone number provided by the funeral director, that of a daughter. Noticing the obituary had mentioned that her mother was a Christian, I asked her daughter when did her Mom become a believer, to which she replied, "Oh, she's pretty much always been a Christian." It is sad that many people think that way, but the Bible tells us we become believers only by accepting the Lord Jesus into our hearts at a point in time and that requires a prayer to be prayed.

The Roman soldier came to Christ, *appealing* or *asking for earnestly*. (Matthew 8:5) Other translations use words like *pleading, asking, and came up in a panic*. Is that our habit of approaching God? The Bible promises, "Draw near to God, and He will draw near to you." (James 4:8)

In his eye-opening book, *Vertical Church*, James Mac-Donald writes:

> *You would see God do a lot more if you would take Him seriously and pray a lot more. Prayer was the single priority that the disciples, when given the chance, asked Jesus to explain in more detail. After watching Him for three years, they didn't ask for a homiletics class to preach better; they didn't request a consultation on the finer points of healing or how to feed five thousand people on a very small budget. All they wanted to know was, 'Lord, teach us to pray.'*[1]

This particular centurion of Caesar was no doubt a man of faith, and therefore boldly approached Jesus, the self-proclaimed Son of God.

We also see that the centurion understood authority. Being a leader himself, this military officer was accustomed to giving commands which were always carried out. All he had to do was speak the word and soldiers obeyed. This Roman leader was fully persuaded that Jesus was One with authority, authority over disease (Matthew 8:1-3), authority over danger (Matthew 8:23-27), and authority over demons (Matthew 8:28-32). Most people healed by Christ received such by offering a leprous hand or touching the hem of His garment. In this particular situation, the Roman soldier knew that only a word from the Christ would suffice. He was one who understood authority.

My wife went to Florida on a "ladies' spring break" trip with two women in our congregation, leaving me home with Dolly, our Golden Retriever. On one of those nights, I invited three of the men from the church over to our house. One's wife and another's girlfriend were on the trip with Sandie, and my other friend's wife was attending a baby shower. Our big plan for the evening was to consume a couple of big pizzas and watch black and white Abbott and Costello movies. It doesn't get much better than that!

Before my guests arrived, I ran to Walmart and pur-chased three big 2-liter bottles of soft drinks, then I picked up the pizzas. When I returned home and put the bags of drinks on the kitchen counter, the Dr. Pepper fell out of the bag, bounced off the floor, and rolled about five feet until it crashed into the baseboard. I picked it up and put it back on the counter with the Coke and the Diet DP. My friends arrived, we had prayer in the living room, then we went into the kitchen, and I might add, the newly semi-remodeled kitchen. I had forgotten about the Dr. Pepper's fall, at least until one young man twisted its cap, spewing DP on himself and the kitchen counter and floor. Grabbing paper towels, I began to soak up the spilled soda. Another of my friends grabbed the sprayer of our new kitchen faucet, intending to spray the drink off of the top of the sink. Instead, the spray-er was facing his direction and he promptly sprayed himself as well as the kitchen floor! Then the other guy comes into the kitchen to offer assistance and accidentally kicks Dolly's water bowl, splashing water all over the floor!

Without a doubt, I had completely lost control! No longer did I possess any authority in my own kitchen! My wife phoned later that night and when I told her all that had happened, she told me those three guys could not come over again without adult supervision! No authority!

It's quite interesting that the centurion in our story clearly understood the power of Christ, while others in the same narrative were merely flabbergasted! Mr. Centurion was not so much amazed at the healing of his slave-boy as much as he understood the authority of the Son of God! On another occasion, a paralyzed man was lowered on a cot through a hole in the roof as Jesus was preaching in a standing-room-only house. With only a word, our Lord healed the man and ordered him to pick up his bed and walk. Don't you know that jam-packed crowd cleared an aisle for him as that healed man, cot tucked under his arm, marched right out of that place! Luke tells us that "they were all amazed, and they glorified God and were filled with fear, saying, 'We have seen strange things today!'" (Luke 5:26)

Do you ever see *strange things* happen in your church or at your home or even in your own individual life? I'm speaking of strange things in a good kind of way. Do you witness happenings in your life that can only be explained as a *God-thing?* You should! If you and I are children of the King, we should see strange things happen in our lives at the Hand of Almighty God on a regular basis.

There's one last thing about the faith-filled Roman centurion. He exercised great faith. He displayed it. It was showing. It's worthy to note that the soldier was a Gentile, and Jesus was a Jew. A Gentile's home was considered unclean to a Jew, therefore Jesus was forbidden by law to enter the centurion's house ... but He was going to do so anyway. (Matthew 8:7) The centurion, however, had enough faith to believe Jesus could heal even from a distance. (Matthew 8:8) So the Roman soldier did something himself prior to his servant's healing, he exercised faith.

In order to witness the power of God, one must do something, one must take action, and that action is that of exercising faith. The priests carrying the Ark of the Covenant had to step into the water before the river divided! Abraham changed his address, moving his entire family and all his belongings, unaware of his destination! Joshua marched around Jericho seven times before the walls of the city collapsed! Elijah sat by a drying brook during a drought, trusting ravens, dirty scavenger birds, for his food! A blind man went and washed in the pool of Siloam before he received his sight! We cannot miss the all important lesson here: We absolutely must crawl out on a limb of faith if we want to observe a mighty moving of God!

But I don't have much faith! you may be thinking. That's perfectly alright—as we've already learned, just use what you have! Dr. Bill Sullivan wrote: "... faith is like a mustard seed and, though it is very small, it will grow and flourish into a great garden plant, and in time it will develop into a mighty faith that can even move mountains into the midst of the sea."[2] The Dad who brought his ailing and disturbed boy to Jesus for healing said that he believed, but he then pleaded with Jesus, "Help my unbelief!"

If anyone has faith, it should be the church crowd! Yet Jesus says people will come from all over and sit down at the banquet table of God, while "heirs of the Kingdom" will be cast into outer darkness! (Matthew 8:11-12) Wow. He had previously said in the Sermon on the Mount that not everyone who calls Him *Lord* will make it to heaven but only the ones who are obedient to His teachings. It sounds as if good folk will be lost from the church pew because being a radical disciple of the Lord Jesus is serious business.

What did our centurion-friend do? He exercised faith. He believed and expected. He told Jesus to just say the word and he was most confident the healing would take place, even down the road. (Matthew 8:8) What happened? Verse 13 tells us that Jesus did indeed speak the word and the servant was made well at that same moment, and it was all because of the centurion's faith. The Bible says, "When Jesus heard it, He marveled, and said to those who followed, 'Assuredly, I say to you, I have not found such great faith, not even in Israel!'" (Matthew 8:10)

Only twice in the Gospels did Jesus marvel: One time was, of course, here in Matthew 8 at the enormous faith of the Gentile military leader. The other time was at the great unbelief of the Jews in Mark 6:6. Matthew recorded two "Gentile" miracles in his gospel: The healing of the centurion's slave and the healing of the daughter of the Syrophoenician woman. In both cases, our Lord was amply impressed with *such great faith.*

Might I ask you a personal question? How is your faith? I'm speaking of your own personal belief in God, Who He is and what He can do. The Apostle Paul said that he had fought a good fight and that he was coming to the finish line, all because of his great faith. (2 Timothy 4:7) It took faith for Paul to become a Christian. It took faith for him to survive stonings and shackles and shipwrecks. It took such great faith for the courageous apostle to hold steady in such days of difficulty and danger.

Why is it so complicated to live the Christian life? Why is it that we believers are so often merely a short step away from throwing in the towel? It's simply because Satan is out to shipwreck our faith! After an explanation of the events of 9/11 in New York City, Jack Graham informs us, "… we have an enemy whose power is far greater than that of even the darkest, deadliest terrorist. The threat is greater. The stakes are higher. The costs are more personal. But the first step in defeating Satan is the same first step required to defeat terrorists. We must be aware of the war."[3]

Dolly was our Golden Retriever. She lived to be 13 years old. She was such a good girl. Whenever she needed to go out during the night, she would come to my or Sandie's side of the bed, sit, and stare at us. She was only inches away. She didn't cry or whimper. She never made a peep. She just stared and waited for us to wake up. Several times I've had a strange feeling that eyes were watching me and I would open my eyes to suddenly realize I was face to snout with our pup. I'd ask, "Dolly, do you need to go outside?" She would respond by backing up and looking very excited, so I would get up and take her downstairs to the back door. I don't know how long she might have waited for one of us to awaken. I do know that she didn't make a sound because she had faith that if she would keep looking into our faces, we'd eventually come to her aid.

It is my personal belief that if I will approach the Father, face to Face, and wait in His presence with faith that He is going to respond. He will take notice and begin to work in my life. The sky's the limit on what God can do but only if He sees our total confidence in Him. For what do you need **SUCH GREAT FAITH?**

CHAPTER TWELVE

SO HOW DO I GET MORE FAITH?

> The apostles said to the Lord,
> "Increase our faith!"
> (Luke 17:5, ESV)

"RUNNING LOW ON FAITH? STOP IN FOR A FILL-UP," the sign read outside the front door of the little church. If only it were that easy. Our friends at this particular house of worship were apparently implying that we can get to a place on our spiritual journey where our proper and needed amount of faith has been depleted. The sign's message also alludes to the fact that when that happens, one is in big time trouble, spiritually, and should hurry inside the church where one's faith can be replenished.

The church I pastor recently held a Faith Promise Convention weekend, a time for special services, including a Saturday night banquet, for receiving pledges to finance our mission needs for the fiscal year. Our guest speaker was a missionary medical doctor who came from the Nazarene hospital in Papua, New Guinea to share her story of God's faithfulness and to challenge our people. Our goal for prayer-driven pledges was $45,000.

Without any trouble, we had met our pledge goals in the past and all the needed funds had been received from our generous congregation throughout the years. The last few Faith Promise Conventions, however, were held in the Spring—usually March or April. This time it was early February. Our annual convention is scheduled according to dates a missionary speaker has available. This particular physician was on furlough during the first couple of weeks in February so we grabbed her, settling for an early event. It had also been a brutal winter for most of the country with record-breaking snowfalls around the Indianapolis area. We had already cancelled services more than once due to the weather and on this particular weekend, a few churches in town had already posted closings on the TV news.

So we had several things against a successful Faith Promise weekend: It was early in the year, as opposed to March or April. It was a snowy Sunday morning in New Castle with below freezing temperatures. I knew some of our most faithful people would be hindered from coming due to the inclement weather. Really not the best time to have a Faith Promise Rally.

Concerned about the possibility of missing our goal, several thoughts raced through my mind throughout the busy weekend. *We could lower our financial goal this year— perhaps $35,000, rather than $45,000. We could insert pledge cards in the worship folder for the next couple of Sundays in order to catch those who were absent. That way, it wouldn't be humiliating for anyone when we fail to meet our goal.* But as quickly as those pitiful ponderings entered my mind, so did another thought—*Oh you of little faith!*

The decision was made to leave it the way it was. Regardless of the attendance, we would have the missionary make her presentations on the dates and times as scheduled. After her Sunday morning message, pledge cards would be distributed, collected, and delivered to a couple of people operating two adding machines down front. What's more, we would keep a running total and the amounts would be projected on a screen for all to see. We would know the faithfulness of our folk before we tried to beat a path to the restaurants for dinner.

They came, scattering all across the sanctuary that had several empty pews due to the absence of many. She spoke, using colorful slides to display her work in New Guinea, making our people aware of the need. And God blessed, making His Presence real and whispering into the ears and hearts of our people, telling them how much He wants to give through them. Within minutes, the first total was flashed on the screen—$25.000! In about the same amount of time, the new and final figure appeared—$53,410! We had pledged beyond our goal within a matter of minutes! There wasn't even enough time to put the pledges up in increments to make it more exciting!

I'll admit, my faith was not very high that Sunday morning. If we could have only had these services scheduled for later in the year—when the weather would be better—when more people would be in attendance—when it wouldn't be an embarrassment to post those figures for all to see.

As we notice the mammoth mountains that always seem to surround us, it is often difficult to muster up enough faith to overcome them. The Apostle Paul certainly had his share of trouble. He wrote of his experiences: "We are hard pressed on every side, but not crushed; perplexed, but not in despair; persecuted, but not abandoned; struck down, but not destroyed." (2 Corinthians 4:8-9, NIV) Commenting on God's perpetual protection, Brother Paul says that we are to never ever lose heart or pitch-in the towel. "So we're not giving up." (2 Corinthians 4:16, MSG) Though I'm sure it would be of benefit, the mere attendance of a worship service as suggested on the afore-mentioned church sign probably won't work any magic.

Remember the little boy in need of healing in Matthew's gospel, chapter nine? Aware of the miraculous experiences that had taken place at the anointed hands of the apostles, the boy's Dad presented his son to those very disciples of the Lord Jesus, but all were surprised when they were not able to help. About that time, Jesus Himself descended from the Mount of Transfiguration and heard the bickering between the father and His right-hand men. After learning what had happened (or I should say, what had not happened) and gathering a little bit of medical history, Jesus told the boy's father that all things were possible if one truly believed (Mark 9:23). That's when the Dad immediately fessed-up, "I believe; help my unbelief!" (Mark 9:24, ESV) Eugene Peterson translates, "I believe. Help me with my doubts!" (The Message)

Now, you and I may be tempted to frown upon the father for his blunt admission, but we have no reason to do so, nor should we. This good man was honestly verbalizing what most, if not all, of us could declare as well. *Lord, I do believe, but way down deep inside of me there is still a tad of doubt. I am well aware that God can do anything, but way down in the crevices of my soul, I wonder if He can take care of this particular predicament, this time. That's where I need help!*

So how, then, does one obtain a sufficient amount of faith? I mean, enough trust to anticipate God's hand at work in one's life? That being the legitimate concern of the disciples of Jesus, they point-blank appealed to the Master, "Increase our faith." (Luke 17:5) In studying the original language of that statement, we see that the Greek word for *increase* is in the imperative mood which means this is a command or at least, a polite request. These boys were serious with their asking, desperately in need of a stronger dose of miracle-believing faith. Haven't we all stood in their sandals?

Jesus answered them with an astounding proclamation about having faith the size of a mustard seed, which they knew to be one terribly tiny kernel. He was saying that it doesn't take an enormous amount of faith to move mountains. We only need to use however much faith we already possess, even if considered to be on the low side.

Without a doubt, you and I have faith. If you didn't, you wouldn't be reading this book. If I didn't, I wouldn't be sitting outside a Starbucks in Orange County, California typing these words. If we didn't, we would never go to church or pray or read our Bibles or pay tithe. As a matter of fact, if we were totally faithless, we couldn't even be saved or sanctified or even get a smile from God. (Hebrews 11:6) Nevertheless, it may be that we still feel the need to be moving mountains while our well of belief seems to be running dry.

Every Sunday morning as I back the car out of our driveway, I make a very serious statement out loud, "It's going to be a good one today!" Sandie usually responds with, "That's what you said last week!" Andrea Kesterson, the daughter we never had, lived with us for a few months of her college career. As we would leave for church on Sunday, she always liked to beat me to it and make the statement before I could get it out. Why do I make that weekly declaration on the way to Sunday School and worship? It's because I'm preparing my mind for a great day in worship. I'm clearing my mind of all doubts and focusing on the power of the Holy Spirit to do whatever He wants to do in that service that morning. I'm leaving no room for Satan to interfere with what God wants to accomplish. I'm making myself available to God to help me to preach with fervency and fire. As a matter of fact, my prayer before I preach is to always ask the Holy Spirit to help me to preach *with fervency and fire!* Obviously, I think it helps at times to talk to ourselves and cheer ourselves on.

One of the giants in my life was Dr. Bill Sullivan. He was one who believed in me, so much that when he was District Superintendent of the North Carolina District Church of the Nazarene, he offered Sandie and me our first church assignment which we prayerfully accepted. Fresh out of college, I pastored Southeast Church of the Nazarene in Greensboro, North Carolina for a month by myself. Then Sandie and I were married and she joined me after a Disney World honeymoon.

Dr. Sullivan was a man of tremendous faith. That's the only way he could have planted all the new churches that were started in North Carolina. I'll never forget the first report I heard him present to the district assembly. He had titled it, "A Sprig of Green." Wearing a green suit, Dr. Sullivan preached to the district delegates and friends of the assembly about growing the Church in North Carolina by finding the right locations and starting new works. Filled with enormous faith, he soon accepted an election and moved to Kansas City to lead Evangelism Ministries for our denomination. While there, he started "K-Church," the School of Large Church Management, a three year program to train Nazarene pastors to reach one thousand people in either membership or attendance. As I finish this chapter as well as bring this book to a close, allow me to borrow from Dr. Sullivan's classic book, *Ten Steps to Breaking the 200 Barrier*. He presents six ways to increase one's faith.

READ ABOUT FAITH IN BIBLE PASSAGES

Quoting the Old Testament prophet, Habakkuk, Paul admonished his Roman readers to live by faith (Romans 1:17). Reading the stories of Abraham, Moses, Elijah, and Joshua will inspire us. Reading about the miracles of Jesus and those people involved will excite us. Reading great chapters on faith such as Matthew 21 and 22 will encourage us. Reading powerful passages like Mark 9:23-24; 11:23-24; Luke 17:5;

Acts 3:16; and Hebrews 11:1 will challenge us. Nothing can affect us like the Holy Scriptures because they are God-breathed.

I think I have already alluded to the fact that I like to read. If someone asked me about a hobby, I suppose reading would be it. I love to read books about God, Jesus, the Holy Spirit, faith, pastoral ministry, preaching, and church growth. I enjoy reading commentaries and other publications that take the Word of God and break it down into understandable meaning. Recently, however, I have been convicted about reading books about the Bible instead of reading the Bible itself. It's much like knowing about Jesus but not knowing Jesus.

John Wesley once said of himself that he was "homo unis libri—a man of one book" Then, in order to avoid any confusion, he said, "O give me that book! At any price, give me the book of God!" Well, Wesley lived a long time ago. Does anyone feel that way today? Pastor Rick Warren wrote, "You can't love God unless you know him, and you can't know him without knowing his Word. The Bible says God 'revealed himself to Samuel through his word.' God still uses that method today."[1] (Warren, *The Purpose Driven Life*)

READ ABOUT FAITH IN FAITH-INSPIRING BOOKS

There are powerful biographies and autobiographies of great people of faith like George Muiller, Phineas Bresee, and Billy Graham. As a young pastor, I read Wesley Tracy's book, *When Adam Clark Preached, People Listened*, a publication that inspired me to attempt to become a great preacher, just like Adam Clark. I purchased Carl Bangs' work on Dr. Bresee at our denomination's General Assembly and finished reading the book before returning home. It both stirred and challenged me. Dr. Bresee was a great pioneer of faith and that comes out loud and clear in that book. As we read these works on such great people of faith, a bit of that faith is passed on to us.

READ THE STORIES OF GREAT CHURCHES

Jim Cymbala's books, *Fresh Wind, Fresh Fire* and *Fresh Faith* tell the story of how God took the 30-person Brooklyn Tabernacle housed in a run-down building in 1971 and grew it into the church that ministers to thousands of people today. Read about how God spoke to a young preacher named Rick Warren and told him to plant a church in the Saddleback community of southern California. That church now reaches thousands of people each week with satellite churches posted in various places.

That's not to mention Andy Stanley's church in Georgia or Willow Creek near Chicago or David Jeremiah's congregation at Shadow Mountain. In reading the histories of these great churches, it won't take you long to discover a key ingredient to their growth is faith.

LOOK FOR EXAMPLES OF MOUNTAIN-MOVING FAITH

Dr. Sullivan says to "Watch for those people whose lives indicate they have the gift of faith."[2] That person may be a pastor or a layperson. He or she may be your neighbor or a relative. Look for him, find her, track them down, and be inspired and learn from those individuals. Those are the kinds of people you and I want to be around. They are the ones we want to surround ourselves with, to rub off on to us. They are the ones who can mentor you and me until we become persons of powerful faith.

While pastoring at Wilmington, North Carolina, our second time in the state, the district superintendent scheduled a pastors' meeting at a resort on the coast near our city. Since I was the host pastor, I was given the privilege of picking up our speaker at the airport. Dr. John Knight was then a General Superintendent in the Church of the Nazarene, and he was also a gifted preacher. I picked him up and drove slowly from the airport to the hotel, picking his brain all the way. Three days later I took him back to the airport, taking the long way, as I learned even more from him on the skills of preaching. We should take as many opportunities as we can to glean great truths from great people of faith.

LISTEN TO PEOPLE OF GREAT FAITH

It may be on a podcast, a DVD, on TV, or in some live venue, but whenever the opportunity is there to hear a person of inspiration speak, take advantage. As a Trevecca student, I once drove about 200 miles roundtrip to hear Evangelist Chuck Millhuff preach. I've driven other distances to hear general superintendents or pastors or evangelists preach and I have been inspired by their Spirit-anointed messages. Today we even have the advantage of hearing sermons of great preachers on church web sites. As a matter of fact, my messages are now on our church website and I find it interesting that most of the listeners are from out-of-state. Whenever you listen to great orators of God's Word, pay particular attention to personal definitions of faith and what these ministers do to keep their hope alive.

ASK GOD TO INCREASE YOUR FAITH

The Bible says, "Every good gift and every perfect gift is from above, and comes down from the Father of lights, with whom there is no variation or shadow of turning." (James 1:17) One of those good and perfect gifts is such great faith. This is exactly what the disciples requested and they were not turned away. It's absolutely permissible to pray about faith.

So how do I get more faith? Well, it won't be by running into some worship service of a well meaning church, as one may be instructed from a sign on a lawn. It will be, however, by reaching within ourselves to grab as much faith as we can find and reaching out to a God Who is bigger than what's the matter!

CHAPTER THIRTEEN

The TEST of FAITH

> ... *God tested Abraham*
>
> (Genesis 22:1, NRSV)

M y plan was to end this book with twelve chapters, however, a recent stint in the hospital has led me to add one more, a chapter on "The Test of Faith." Whether it was grade school or grad school, I was never a good test-taker. Permit me to write papers all day long, but please don't give me an exam. Does it bother you or even surprise you that the Scripture tells us, "God tested Abraham?" (Genesis 22:1, NRSV)

Abram, before he was called Abraham, had his share of tests from the beginning. There was the "family test," where God had called him to leave his homeland, his loved ones, all that was familiar, for a new land he had never seen. (Genesis 1) Then there was the "famine test," one that he had failed, for he doubted and looked to Egypt for help. (Genesis 12) The "fellowship test" saw Abraham giving Lot first choice in the pastureland (Genesis 13) and in the "fight test" he defeated the kings. (Genesis 14). It was the "fortune test" where Abraham refused all of Sodom's wealth. (Genesis 14) The "fatherhood test" was another one botched, for Abe had doubted he would ever be a dad and took matters into his own hands, begetting a child by a slave-girl. (Genesis 16) The "farewell test" was the one that broke Abraham's heart, sending away his first-born son, Ishmael. (Genesis 21) So the Bible teaches us that in the "School of Faith" there are various assessments along the way to see how well we are spiritually.

It is important that we distinguish between *trials* and *temptations.* Temptations come from desires within us (James 1:14), while trials come from the Lord, Who has a special purpose for everyone. Warren Wiersbe wrote, "Temptations are used by the devil to bring out the worst in us, but trials are used by the Holy Spirit to bring out the best in us."[1] (Wiersbe)

One of my favorite chapters in the Bible is the eighth chapter of Matthew, one that displays the awesome power of Almighty God through His Son, Jesus Christ. We first find Jesus healing a leper, actually touching him, an act that was totally forbidden. He then heals a soldier's servant— from a distance. Next He goes into a back bedroom in the house of Mark and heals Peter's mother-in-law of a fever. The former tax collector then explains how Jesus healed crowds of people, even casting evil spirits out of those who were demon-possessed.

Then it happens: After all of these tremendous acts of power, Jesus persuades His disciples to get into a boat with Him for a short sail across the lake. (It was a test!) While the vessel is out on a joy cruise, a storm blows up and the little boat is tossed all over the water. The disciples are afraid for their lives—just after all those displays of the godly power of Jesus! That's why His remark to them was, "Why are you fearful, O you of little faith?" (Matthew 8:26, NKJV) I don't believe God causes bad things to happen but I do believe there are times when God tests us to see what we know and what we believe, as is seen in Genesis 22:1-8, the test of Abraham's faith.

We're all familiar with the story. God had promised Abram a child, even in the later years of his and his wife's lives (Abraham was 99 and Sarah was a decade younger). A son, in fact, is born just as promised and a dozen or so years later, God tells the father to sacrifice his boy on a mountain. Abraham had been walking with God for over fifty years. In his book, *Perfectly Imperfect: Character Sketches From the Old Testament,* David Busic points out the fact that Abraham knew God's voice. He had heard His Voice promise to make him a blessing. He had heard His Voice promise the inheritance of Canaanland. He had also heard that Voice promise to give him a son. Dr. Busic goes on to explain how Abraham knew the command, *Go!* Now with the impending sacrifice of Isaac, God once again gives the same command in Genesis 22:2, the same Hebrew word for *Go!*[2] (Busic)

Why does it not surprise us that Abraham's answer to God was *Yes?!* He cuts the wood by himself, takes the boy (who probably was a young man by now) and a couple of servants, and heads for Mount Moriah, a fifty-mile trek from Beersheba. Knowing this was something he could only do alone, Abraham left his servants along the way, and he and Isaac proceeded to their destination. But before leaving his men, Abraham made the statement that *we* will worship on the mountain and then return. (Genesis 22:5) Abraham apparently believed that once he sacrificed his boy, God would raise him from the dead. We read in the New Testament, "By faith Abraham, when he was tested, offered up Isaac … his only begotten son, of whom it was said, 'In Isaac your seed shall be called,' concluding that God was able to raise him up, even from the dead." (Hebrews 11:17-19, NKJV)

Abraham gets the altar and fire ready and Isaac begins to inquire about the missing lamb. His Dad assures him that God will provide the sacrifice. No doubt with tears in his eyes, Abraham binds his son and places him on the altar, without a struggle. That boy had watched his Dad, had believed in him, and trusted him, along with his God. This story makes me think of my own Dad. Before he died at the age of 54, he struggled every day with diabetes and kidney disease but never flinched in his faith. He is still remembered to this day by many for his inspiring walk with the Lord Jesus.

Now to the reason for this added chapter. Physically, I had been experiencing some problems for several weeks. After discussing it with my personal physician, he and I had decided to see how things go over the next few months. My problem, however, rapidly progressed. I decided to call my doctor on a Monday morning, only to discover that he was on vacation. On Tuesday I made the five hour drive to Cleveland, Ohio and found my hotel room. I was there for the brain surgery of one of my church attendees, scheduled for the next morning at the Cleveland Clinic, as mentioned in another chapter. That Tuesday night I had trouble, not to mention all day Wednesday as I sat with a family. Driving home late Wednesday night, I was in much pain. Fully aware that my doctor was gone, the next morning I called his office and asked to see one of his partners. I was granted an appointment and this particular physician diagnosed an infection and prescribed a couple of drugs.

Even then, things became worse over the next week so I called my doctor's office again, relieved to know my doctor was now back from his trip. However, I was told that there were no openings until the next week. Realizing I was in trouble, I texted a doctor in my church, "I'm in a world of hurt! Anyway you can see me?" Within minutes he responded, telling me to come to his office immediately. After taking one look at me, my friend sent me across the street to the hospital. I was told to not check in with admissions as one would normally do, but to go straight to a unit on the second floor, where my wife and I found they were waiting on us, just as the doctor ordered.

Please understand, being a pastor, I had no time to be in a hospital. It was a late Thursday afternoon and Sunday was a-comin.' I really needed to finish up my sermons. I also had a committal service at a local cemetery on Saturday afternoon. I had places to go, people to see, and things to do, all in the Name of Jesus! This was no time for me to be down, but I'll confess, I was one sick preacher. The next four days were spent in Henry County Hospital in New Castle, Indiana, a facility where I frequently made calls but this time I was on the other side of the bed rail. Ct-scans revealed I did indeed have a severe infection, and I soon found myself tethered to the bed with IV bags of powerful antibiotics.

The first evening I ran a fever and hallucinated most of the night. The second night was one with nightmares. This was certainly no fun experience. Then on Saturday night I was wide awake and stared at the wall until 4:15 a.m. That's when I started hearing "the voice," but it for sure was not God's voice. The thought that hit me again and again was, *For over thirty years I had preached that 'God is bigger!' Where is my God now? He suddenly doesn't seem to be so big!*

Can anyone relate? Do you know what I'm talking about? You surrender your life to Jesus, walk with Him and talk with Him, live your life according to God's holy Will, then out of the blue you find yourself in a royal mess with God seemingly a thousand miles away! That's where I was.

I soon began to think about the test of Abraham in Genesis 22, and I wanted to read about it but since I hadn't planned on being hospitalized, I had not brought my Bible. I am well aware of the hospital Bible in the drawer, but I honestly didn't think of it and even if I had, I was unable to reach it. Contacting my friend, Brad, I asked him to grab one of my own Bibles out of my study the next morning at church and to bring it on Sunday afternoon. Until then, I was on my own.

Around 7 a.m. Sunday morning, I turned the TV on and found Dr. David Jeremiah's *Turning Point* program from his church near San Diego. I like to listen to Dr. Jeremiah and even attended services at his church once at Shadow Mountain. He just happened to be preaching on "The Test of Abraham." Later I looked up Genesis 22 in my own Bible and read about Abraham's famous test of faith. Once out of the hospital, I had a few weeks to recuperate on the living room sofa. Picking up David Busic's new book that I had started to read a week or so earlier, I found the next chapter to be on, of all things, Abraham's test of faith. Do you think the Lord was trying to teach me something?

Like Abraham, I too knew the Voice! I had heard that Voice call me to Christianity on a Sunday night, November 5, 1972. I had heard that Voice three years later calling me to entire sanctification. I heard that Voice in a wrestling ring in LaGrange, Georgia in 1975 calling me to preach, and a few weeks later I heard that Voice calling me to go to college, six years after high school.

I also knew God's command. It had always been to *go* and I would in turn follow. His command was to go and preach the Gospel anywhere. Over the years, I've preached in Protestant churches and in Catholic churches. I've preached in college and seminary chapels, on the beach, and on funeral home lawns. I've preached in mortuaries, grave yards, nursing homes, in parking lots, and at rescue missions. I've preached in many cities and states across America and, like a real, live missionary, I've proclaimed the Word with rolled-up sleeves under a spinning ceiling fan in San Juan, Puerto Rico. I had always tried to be faithful to the Call of God on my life. And now I was out of the hospital but in a recliner at home with orders not to do anything, as if I had the energy to try.

During those days of convalescence, Sandie shared a devotional with me that was hers for that particular day:

> *"Accept each day as it comes to you. Do not waste your time and energy wishing for a different set of circumstances. Instead, trust Me enough to yield to My design and purposes."[3]*

I was definitely feeling like this illness was an unwanted test of my faith. I missed three whole Sundays at church. On the next two Sundays, Pastor Andrew Hall, my capable youth pastor, filled the pulpit in the morning and I attempted preaching in the evenings, but I was awfully weak the first Sunday night and really overdid it. The next week I was a bit stronger but still not ready to blaze any revival trails. A week or so later, I had my appointment with my specialist who told me I wasn't where he wanted me to be, but the good news was that I was making slow progress.

As I write this chapter, I am recuperating for a week at our son and daughter-in-law's place in southern California. I'm happy to announce that I think I'm about ready to preach holiness once again. Though I would never blame God for my recent illness, I do believe that He can take the bad and turn it into good. That fact is made pretty clear in Paul's letter to the Philippians.

The apostle had been arrested for his faith and writes from a filthy, rat-infested Roman jail cell. He doesn't know what is going to happen next. He could be executed at any moment and he understands that, but at the same time, he could also be released. And the most unusual thing about all of this is that whatever happened would be fine for St. Paul! He wrote, "I am torn between the two: I desire to depart and be with Christ, which is better by far; but it is more necessary for you that I remain in the body." (Philippians 1:23-24, NIV) Paul knew that, should he be allowed to live, he could win more people to Christ. He also realized that if he died, he would go directly to be with Jesus, which was his goal in life. Either way, he wins! Therefore the apostle said that he was "torn between the two." My favorite translation of that phrase is the King James Version: "I am in a strait betwixt two."

Paul also points out the fact that even though he had fallen into rough times, God was turning the bad into good. One would think with the number one evangelist being jailed, the preaching of the gospel would come to a screeching halt. On the contrary, other preachers outside the jail were preaching the message of Jesus. It seems that Paul's imprisonment had encouraged some ministers who had become somewhat lackadaisical in their ministry. All of a sudden, they had a brand new fire to preach the gospel of the Lord Jesus! At the same time, there were some phony preachers who were "preaching" to ridicule Paul but the apostle said that was okay because at least the Name of Jesus was being lifted. (Philippians 1:18) God was taking the bad and changing it into good. The trials of the Apostle Paul were glorifying the Lord.

Well, let's get back to Abraham and Isaac, the story of a father who was willing to sacrifice his own son because He believed God had told him to do so. Does that story sound familiar?—it should! God the Father sent His one and only

Son, Jesus, the One He loved, and sacrificed Him for you and me. (John 3:16) Paul wrote, "He who did not spare his own Son, but gave him up for us all." (Romans 8:32) Jesus even carried the very wood upon which He died up the hill to Calvary, just as Isaac had done.

Whether it's the test of Abraham's faith or the test of yours or mine, God will always provide, as long as we are faithful to His Voice. That's why He is a God Who can be trusted, even with our lives. Dr. Busic challenges us:

> "The greatest test of our faith is not letting go of our sin, our guilt, and our pain. Who wants to hang on to those things? The greatest test of our faith is whether I can trust God with what is most dear to me. Will I even offer my Isaac completely into the hands of God?"[4]

So it comes down to this: What is your "Isaac?" It may be your job, your career, your ambition in life. Does it mean the world to you? Is that what you are all about, climbing the corporate ladder, striving to get to the top? It may be that you can't even go to church on a regular basis because you work so many hours. Perhaps it's money. Once you get more of it, you just want even more than what you have. You may tithe or you may not, but either way, money has become your god.

It may be that family is number one to you. I will agree that family should be important, but second only to God. Jesus said, "He who loves father or mother more than Me is not worthy of Me. And he who loves son or daughter more than Me is not worthy of Me." (Matthew 10:37) He also said, "If anyone comes to Me and does not hate his father and mother, wife and children, brothers and sisters, yes, and his own life also, he cannot be My disciple." (Luke 14:26) Was Jesus really saying we should hate our family? Of course not. Jesus was acknowledging how we love our families with a tremendous amount of love but that such love should "appear" as hate when compared with how much we love and adore and cherish Almighty God.

Your "Isaac" may be one of a number of other things. "Isaac" represents what is most important to you. The question is, are you willing to give it to God? Are you willing to let go of it and sacrifice it to the One Who loves you so much that He sacrificed His one and only Son, and all because of His love for you? You and I owe Him so much.

So how can we do all that's required, all that's expected? My puny little sacrifice seems so small, so useless. It's only by faith. Paul wrote to the Roman believers, "a man is justified by faith." (Romans 3:28, NKJV) I present to Him my all, my everything, with a fervent faith that He accepts my gift. The Christian life is a life of trust, of belief, of faith and at times, we are put to the test. He wants to see how we really feel about Him. This is one test we cannot fail to pass, the test of *Such Great Faith!*

CONCLUSION

YOUR FAITH

> *But you, dear friends,*
> *build yourselves up*
> *in your most holy faith*
> (Jude 20 NIV)

Sandie and I took our seats on the plane, she by the window and I was in the center. A middle-aged lady soon claimed the aisle seat on my left. As we taxied to the runway, the stranger made it known to us that she disliked flying. I noticed as we made our way down the runway with increasing speed that she was making heavy breathing sounds, much like she was hyperventilating. I also saw that with one hand, she grabbed the armrest with a death-grip, then with the other hand, she did the same thing to the back of the seat in front of her. My fear was that next she would grab hold of me!

Once the jet had leveled off in the air, a conversation began between the three of us. She again spoke of her fear of flying and that her husband had instructed her not to grab the person next to her. Our new friend told us that once she was on a plane sitting next to a priest and he assured her that they were going to be alright. That seemed to give her some solace. I then told her, "Well, I'm not a priest, but I AM a pastor." Her reply of relief: "Then I picked the right seat!"

We all laughed but the truth is, it's not a laughing matter. One cannot live their life relying on a priest or a pastor next to them, nor the faith of anyone else. Our faith cannot be in a *someone* but it must be in the Creator Himself.

I've done a lot of reminiscing in this book, looking back on moments in my own life when faith became reality, something that grew until the miraculous happened and God was glorified. I've gone from accepting Christ as my personal Savior, to hearing a still small voice in a wrestling ring, to seeing mountains move, literally, to feeling the power of God at work when my belief was tested. This has been my story, but isn't it also yours? The faces, situations and circumstances may be different but the God is the same, and the faith—it still begins as something the size of a mustard seed and grows. You, too, can and should experience the power of God in your life on a regular basis.

Today I challenge you to believe God for the impossible. Crawl out on a limb of faith, out on to the tiny branches that may not support your weight. Take a risk. Believe Him for a miracle. Put all your trust in the only One Who can catch you, should you fall. Dream some big dreams. Allow God to be God. Become a successful Christian as well as a faithful one. Believe in your heart of hearts that He really is bigger than what's the matter. Put all of this together and you have *Such Great Faith*.

NOTES

Introduction: Whatever Happened to Faith?

[1] Jim Cymbala, *Fresh Faith* (Grand Rapids, MI: Zondervan Publishing House, 1999), p. 77.
[2] Ibid, p. 11.
[3] Frank Moore, *The Power to Be Free* (Kansas City, MO: Beacon Hill Press, 2005), p. 16.

Chapter 1: Called to Preach in a Wrestling Ring

Tony Evans, *Who is This King of Glory?* (Chicago, IL: Moody Press, 1999), p. 216.
[2] H.B. London & Neil Wiseman, *They Call Me Pastor* (Ventura, CA: Regal Books, 2000) p. 114.

Chapter 2: The Get-Out-on-a-Limb Kind of Faith

Oswald Chambers, *My Utmost For His Highest* (New York City, NY: Dodd, Mead & Company, 1935), p. 151.
[2] Jim Newheiser, *Opening Up Proverbs* (Leominster, UK: Day One Christian Ministries, 2008), p. 61.
[3] H.B. London & Neil Wiseman, *They Call Me Pastor*, (Ventura, CA: Regal Books, 2000) p. 111.

Chapter 3: Faith That Takes a Risk

Answers.com.
[2] W.T. Purkiser, *Exploring Our Christian Faith* (Kansas City, MO: Beacon Hill Press, 1960), p. 27.

[3]Herman's Hermits, *This Door Swings Both Ways,* written by Don Thomas, Estelle Levitt.

[4]Albert J. Lown, *Portraits of Faith,* (Kansas City, MO: Beacon Hill Press, 1981), p. 37.

[5]Bill M. Sullivan, *Ten Steps to Breaking the 200* Barrier (Kansas City, MO: Beacon Hill Press, 1988), p. 33.

Chapter 4: A Little Training From a Little Train

[1]Watty Piper, *The Little Engine That Could* (New York City, NY: The Platt & Munk Co., Inc, 1930).

[2]T.W. Willingham, *Crumbs of Faith, Spiritual Insights, Book 4* (Kansas City, MO: Beacon Hill Press, 1987), p. 45.

Chapter 5: Faith That Moves Mountains

Warren Wiersbe, *The Bible Exposition Commentary* (Wheaton, IL: Victor Books, 1989), p. 142

[2]Dick Eastman, *The Hour That Changes the World* (Grand Rapids, MI: Chosen Books, 2002), pp. 81-82.

Chapter 6: What is Faith?

Billy Graham, *Peace With God* (Waco, TX: Word, 1953), p. 160.

[2]John C. Bowling, *Above All Else* (Kansas City, MO: Beacon Hill Press, 2012), p. 25.

[3]Everett Leadingham, Editor, *I Believe* (Kansas City, MO: Beacon Hill Press, 1994), p. 131.

[4]Gordon E. Jackson & Phyllisee Foust Jackson, *Pathways to Faith* (Nashville, TN: Abingdon Press, 1989), p. 20.

[5]Richard Leslie Parrott, *My Soul Purpose* (Nashville, TN: The Woodland Press, 2009), p. 53.

[6]J.I. Packer, *Growing in Christ* (Wheaton, IL: Crossway Books, 1994), pp. 19-20.

[7]Max Lucado, *3:16* (Nashville, TN: Thomas Nelson, 2007), p. 10.

[8]J.I. Packer, *Growing in Christ* (Wheaton, IL: Crossway Books, 1994), p. 20.

[9]James Spruce, *A Simple Faith* (Kansas City, MO: Beacon Hill Press, 1997), p. 119.

Chapter 7: Believing is Seeing
[1]Jim Cymbala, *Fresh Faith* (Grand Rapids, MI: Zondervan Publishing House, 1999), p. 16.
[2]James MacDonald, *Vertical Church* (Colorado Springs, CO: David C. Cook, 2012), p. 281.

Chapter 8: Jesus Frowns on Faithlessness
Jim Cymbala, *Breakthrough Prayer* (Grand Rapids, MI: Zondervan, 2003), p. 178.
[2]Frank Moore, *The Power to Be Free* (Kansas City, MO: Beacon Hill Press, 2005), p. 16.
[3]H.B. London & Neil Wiseman, *They Call Me Pastor* (Ventura, CA: Regal Books, 2000) p. 111.

Chapter 9: How Much is Enough?
Robert Jamieson, A.R. Fausset, & David Brown, *Commentary Critical and Explanatory on the Whole Bible* (Oak Harbor, WA: Logos Research Systems, Inc., 1997).

Chapter 10: But What If …?
J. Ronald Blue, *Habakkuk, The Bible Knowledge Commentary: An Exposition of the Scriptures*, John F. Walvoord and Roy B. Zuck, Editors (Wheaton, IL: Victor Books, 1983), p. 1511.
[2]Stan Toler, *Stan Toler's Practical Guide for Pastoral* Ministry (Indianapolis, IN: Wesleyan Publishing House, 2007), p. 179
[3]Jack Graham, *Unseen* (Bloomington, MN: Bethany House Publishers, 2013), p. 23.

Chapter 11: Such Great Faith
James MacDonald, *Vertical Church* (Colorado Springs, CO: David C. Cook, 2012), pp. 296-296.

[2]Bill M. Sullivan, *Ten Steps to Breaking the 200 Barrier* (Kansas City, MO: Beacon Hill Press, 1988), p. 32.

[3]Jack Graham, *Unseen* (Bloomington, MN: Bethany House Publishers, 2013), p. 146.

Chapter 12: So How Do I Get More Faith?

Rick Warren, *The Purpose Driven Life* (Grand Rapids, MI: Zondervan, 2002), p. 90.

[2]Bill M. Sullivan, *Ten Steps to Breaking the 200 Barrier* (Kansas City, MO: Beacon Hill Press, 1988), p. 30.

Chapter 13: The Test of Faith

Warren Wiersbe, *Be Obedient* (Colorado Springs, CO: David C. Cook, 2010), p. 108

[2]David Busic, *Perfectly Imperfect* (Kansas City, MO: Beacon Hill Press: 2013), pp. 41-42.

[3]Sarah Young, *Jesus Calling,* (Nashville, TN: Thomas Nelson, 2004), p. 240.

[4]David Busic, *Perfectly Imperfect* (Kansas City, MO: Beacon Hill Press: 2013), pp. 47-48.